Double-Shift Schooling

Double-Shift Schooling

DESIGN AND OPERATION FOR COST-EFFECTIVENESS

Mark Bray
THE UNIVERSITY OF HONG KONG

Commonwealth Secretariat
International Institute for Educational Planning

First edition published 1989 in English under the title *Multiple-Shift Schooling: Design and Operation for Cost-Effectiveness* by the Commonwealth Secretariat and the Unit for Cooperation with UNICEF, UNESCO, Paris. French translation published 1989 by the Unit for Cooperation with UNICEF under the title *La scolarisation à vacations multiples: Conception et mise en œuvre pour un meilleur rapport coût-efficacité.* Khmer translation published 1995 by UNICEF Phnom Penh.

This second edition published 2000 by:

The Commonwealth Secretariat,
Marlborough House,
Pall Mall,
London SW1Y 5HX,
United Kingdom

and

International Institute for Educational Planning/UNESCO,
7–9 rue Eugène-Delacroix,
75116 Paris,
France.

Artwork by William Pang, The University of Hong Kong.

Commonwealth Secretariat ISBN 0 85092 650 5
UNESCO ISBN 92 803 1200 6

May be purchased from:

Publications Department, Commonwealth Secretariat, Marlborough House, Pall Mall, London SW1Y 5HX, United Kingdom.
E-mail: r.jones-parry@commonwealth.int

or

International Institute for Educational Planning/UNESCO,
7–9 rue Eugène-Delacroix, 75116 Paris, France.
E-mail: information@iiep.unesco.org

Price £10.99

Contents

List of Tables

List of Boxes

Foreword

This is the second edition of a book which was first published in 1989. The first edition was widely welcomed, and has been used as a tool for policy-makers and practitioners in a considerable range of countries. We were very pleased when Mark Bray expressed willingness to update and revise the book for re-publication, and anticipate that this edition will be as enthusiastically welcomed as the last.

The book is intended for two main groups of readers. One group comprises policy-makers at national and regional levels, who will be primarily interested in the balance of broad economic, educational and social factors which must be considered when choosing between models for single, double, or even more shifts. The second group embraces practitioners, who will be primarily concerned with such practical matters as staffing and timetabling. In addition to their own dominant concerns, of course members of each group require an understanding of the perspec-tives of the other group. Professionals from both groups can therefore benefit from careful study of the book as a whole.

A few quotations from reviews of the first edition help to portray the flavour not only of that edition but also of this new, revised version. For example, Keith Watson observed that the book is "extremely useful, readable and thought-provoking".[1] This view matched that of others.[2] A.G. Hopkin observed that the systematic presentation of the book "ensures that the content and argument are accessible to anyone broadly interested in education systems and how they operate";[3] and Clive Whitehead described the book as "essential reading for all students of educational planning and administration".[4]

These views were paralleled in an extended commentary in the

---

[1] Keith Watson (1992). Review in *Third World Quarterly*, Vol.13, No.3.

[2] See for example Sunil Behari Mohanty (1989). Review in *Journal of the All India Association for Educational Research*, Vol.1, No.2; M.K. Bacchus (1990). Review in *Canadian and International Education*, Vol.19, No.1; R.P. Singhal (1990). Review in *Indian Education Review*; and Ron Morton (1991). Review in *Educational Review*, Vol.43. No.1.

[3] A.G. Hopkin (1990). Review in *School Organisation*, Vol.10, Nos. 2 and 3.

[4] Clive Whitehead (1989). Review in *Education Research and Perspectives*, Vol.19, No.2.

journal *Education in Asia and the Pacific*.[5] The reviewer recognised that the book was the product of extensive research, and began by applauding the presentation and format:

> "Bray is, by all counts, an accomplished educationist bent on communicating clearly, interestingly and succinctly. The reader benefits from this. Introductory paragraphs cue the reader to what he is about to be told, and once he has written the chapter there are invariably a few lines to summarize what should have been learnt. And in between, the reader is blessed with a tightly written text that only the meanest of editors could boil down any more."

Turning to content, this reviewer praised the way that the booklet presents information in a "kaleidoscopic" way, identifying the different perspectives of administrators, teachers, parents and pupils. For policy-makers and planners, separate chapters focus on the economic, educational and social factors which must be considered; and for school-level practitioners separate chapters focus on school organisation and timetabling, staffing and management, and quality. The reviewer concluded that:

> "This is a book that needs to be put in the hands of as many administrators as possible. By drawing from real experiences it can give them confidence to make bold moves for increasing resource utilization."

We ourselves readily endorse all these positive comments. When the book was first issued in 1989, no practical guide was available on the subject of double-shift schooling. Over a decade later, it remains the case that no comparable work has been prepared by any other author. We are delighted that this second edition makes Mark Bray's book easily available again, and anticipate that it will be of considerable use to policy-makers and practitioners in a wide range of settings.

Cream Wright,
The Commonwealth Secretariat.

Françoise Caillods,
International Institute for Educational Planning.

---

[5] *Education in Asia and the Pacific* (1989-1990), Vol.26.

Acknowledgements

Many people assisted with the first and second editions of this book, providing materials and commenting on drafts. The author especially wishes to thank Emeka Anyanwu, Charles Currin, Anna Dreba, Françoise du Pouget, Godfrey Kleinans, Elsa Leo-Rhynie, Ora Kwo, Neville Postlethwaite, Kenrick Seepersad, Tan Yap Kwang, R. Murray Thomas, and Sheldon Weeks. The first edition was steered through the publication process by Peter Williams at the Commonwealth Secretariat and by Dieter Berstecher at UNESCO's Unit for Cooperation with UNICEF. This second edition has been steered through the publication process by Cream Wright at the Commonwealth Secretariat and by Françoise Caillods at UNESCO's International Institute for Educational Planning. William Pang at the University of Hong Kong prepared the hand-drawn artwork, and Emily Mang provided secretarial support.

Introduction

This book must begin with some comments on focus and definition. The title refers to double-shift schooling. In a double-shift system, schools cater for two entirely separate groups of pupils during a school day. The first group of pupils usually attends school from early morning until mid-day, and the second group usually attends from mid-day to late afternoon. Each group uses the same buildings, equipment and other facilities. In some systems the two groups are taught by the same teachers, but in other systems they are taught by different teachers.

Some education authorities extend this model into a triple-shift system. Three groups of pupils study e.g. from 6.30 am to 10.55 am, from 11.00 am to 3.25 pm, and from 3.30 pm to 7.55 pm. A few education authorities also operate quadruple-shifts, though Chapter 1 will explain that these systems usually have overlapping rather than end-on shifts.

The first edition of this book was entitled *Multiple-Shift Schooling* rather than *Double-Shift Schooling*. This was to make clear at the outset that discussion focused on triple and quadruple shifts as well as on double shifts. However, the term multiple-shift schooling is not so familiar to many practitioners. With this in mind, the title of this second edition has been adjusted to use the more familiar term. The book does discuss not only triple and quadruple shifts but also single shifts. In the process, it analyses the advantages and disadvantages of different types of arrangements. However, the main focus is on double shifts.

Variations in Terminology

Further variations in terminology may also be noted at the outset. Single-shift schools, for example, may also be called:

- single-session schools,
- unisessional schools, and
- full-day schools.

Correspondingly, double-shift schools may also be called:

- double-session schools,
- bisessional schools, and
- half-day schools.

Sometimes the difference in terminology implies a difference in meaning, as noted in Box 1. This requires care when using terms in different contexts. However, in most contexts the terms can be used interchangeably. It is particularly common to interchange the terms 'shift' and 'session'.

Box 1: What's in a Name?

In most contexts, the terms single-session, single-shift, unisessional and full-day can be used interchangeably. The same applies to the terms double-session, double-shift, bisessional and half-day. But this is not always so. Examples from Botswana and Singapore demonstrate the point.

In *Botswana*, the term 'double-session' has been used to describe schools which have different pupils in the mornings and afternoons, but the same number of classroom hours as pupils in single-session schools, and different teachers for each session. 'Half-session' schools have been formed in Botswana with different pupils in the mornings and afternoons but in which total classroom hours are reduced, and the two groups are taught by the same teachers.

In *Singapore*, single-session schools operate on the traditional pattern from 7.30 am to 1.00 pm. They are different from 'full-day' schools, which were an experiment (now abandoned) in the early 1980s. Full-day schools had an extended curriculum, and did not close till 3.30 pm.

These terminological distinctions are not found in all countries. It is therefore necessary to check the precise meanings of terms in different contexts.

Some countries also have evocative unofficial terminologies. In Zimbabwe, double-session schooling is also called 'hot seating' because the school seats are said never to have time to cool down! And staff in Mexico have been known as 'taxi teachers' because many jumped straight into taxis at the end of each morning session in order to teach afternoon sessions elsewhere. In South Africa and Namibia, double-shift schooling is called 'platooning'. This seems to imply a sort of military-style regimentation.

What are the Purposes of Double-Shift Schooling?

The main purpose of double-shift schooling is to increase the supply of school places while avoiding serious strain on the budget. Introduction of double shifts allows a single set of buildings and facilities to serve more pupils. This may be especially important in urban areas, where land is scarce and buildings are expensive. Double-shift schooling has helped many countries to move towards universal primary and secondary education.

Double-shift schooling may also have subsidiary functions:

- Expansion of the number of school places broadens access. This helps governments to achieve goals of social equity.
- Where there is a shortage of teachers, staff may be encouraged to teach in more than one session. Double-shift schooling may enable the authorities to make better use of scarce human resources.
- When staff teach in more than one session, they usually have higher earnings. Double-shift schooling allows teachers to increase their incomes, and reduces the political tension that arises from low basic salaries.
- In many societies, some children are too poor to spend the whole day in school. They cannot afford the school fees, and they cannot afford to lose the incomes they could gain from working. Double-shift schooling reduces costs, so can also reduce school fees. It also allows pupils to work for more hours in the day, and thus to earn money to support themselves and their families while also enrolling in a school. Systems which have evening shifts can cater for pupils who have to work during the day.
- If enrolment rates are already high, double-shift schooling may be introduced to reduce overcrowding. The system can permit reduction of class size, and can also alleviate pressure on sports facilities, libraries, school canteens, etc.

However, multiple-shift schooling may also create problems. The school day, especially in triple-session systems, is often shortened. This implies that quality is being sacrificed for quantity – that pupils are losing some classroom teaching and extra-curricular activities. Also, if teachers work in more than one session, they are likely to be tired. This can cause a further deterioration in quality. And multiple-shift systems are sometimes accused of causing social problems because children are only occupied in school for shorter periods and so have more time to roam around the streets and cause trouble.

In the view of many people, these problems outweigh the benefits. Public opinion often opposes introduction of double shifts on the grounds that the system can save money but creates educational and social problems. However, this book will point out that such opinion is not always valid. Double-shift systems require more careful and balanced consideration than they often receive.

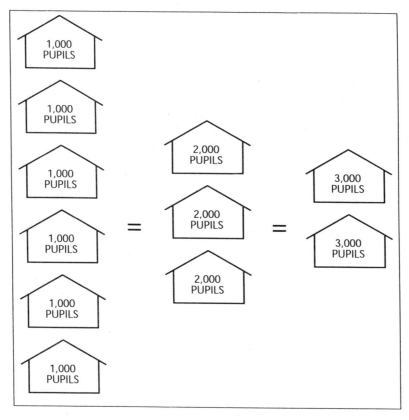

A single-shift system might require six schools to accommodate 6,000 pupils. But a double-shift system would require only three schools, and a triple-shift system would require only two schools. Multiple-shift schooling can permit considerable savings of buildings and land.

Introduction

Box 2: A Model for Poor Countries or Rich Ones?

Double-shift schooling is most common in poor countries. Financial pressures in these countries are so severe that administrators are forced to investigate all ways to minimise costs. But all administrators wish to maximise cost-effectiveness. For this reason, double shifts may also be found in rich countries. Singapore is one example.

PART I

A FRAMEWORK FOR ANALYSIS

Chapter 1

Models for Double-Shift Schooling

International survey reveals many different models for double-shift schooling. This chapter outlines the most common models in order to provide a framework for subsequent analysis.

1. 'End-on' Shifts

Most double-shift systems are of the 'end-on' variety. This means that one group of pupils leaves the school before the next group arrives. This book is mainly concerned with shift systems of this type.

In a double-shift system, the first group of pupils comes early in the morning but leaves at mid-day; and the second group arrives at mid-day but leaves in the late afternoon. In Malaysia, for example, a common pattern is:

- 1st Shift: 7.40 am to 12.40 pm
- 2nd Shift: 1.00 pm to 6.00 pm.

In a triple-shift system, three groups of pupils share one set of buildings and facilities. The pattern in some Zambian schools is:

- 1st Shift: 7.00 am to 10.45 am
- 2nd Shift: 11.00 am to 2.45 pm
- 3rd Shift: 3.00 pm to 6.45 pm.

Because this type of triple-shift can only operate with a very short school day, most authorities only use it as an emergency measure.

2. Overlapping Shifts

Alternatively, shifts may overlap. Students arrive and leave at different times, but at some point are on the school compound together.

Box 3 gives an example of a simple overlapping shift system used in Indonesia. It enabled the school to increase its enrolment and to use its buildings more efficiently while retaining the atmosphere of a single-shift school.

Box 3: Overlapping Shifts – An Indonesian Example

In order to increase utilisation of facilities, Sabelas Maret Secondary School decided to use an overlapping shift system. Through this mechanism, it expanded its enrolment by 25% while still maintaining the atmosphere of a full-day school.

In the old system, the school week had nine lessons a day, Monday to Friday. Even when classrooms were used all the time, they only accommodated 45 lessons per week. The overlapping shift system increased the school day to 11 lessons, allowing the classrooms to accommodate 55 lessons a week. This represented a 22.2% increase in room utilisation. Space for the students when they were all on the compound together was found by using laboratories, workshops, the library, and sports fields (for physical education).

The operation of the shifts was as follows:

- *Shift A:* 9 periods per day, 8.15 am to 3.10 pm, and
- *Shift B:* 9 periods per day, 9.35 am to 4.30 pm.

Both shifts had the same lunch hour, from 12.10 to 1.10 pm. This helped students of each shift to meet each other and to feel part of a single institution. The system required efficient timetabling, but did not cause major problems.

A more complex system of overlapping shifts has been used in Malawi to tackle the problem that many schools have insufficient class-rooms and that some students must study outside. Pupils in Standards (Grades) 3, 4 and 5 only come when pupils in Standards 1 and 2 leave, but pupils in Standards 6, 7 and 8 overlap with both groups. This timetable is presented in Chapter 6.

That chapter also discusses a yet more complicated example: a school in the Philippines which managed even to have *quadruple* overlapping shifts. The school timetable is complex, but the example shows that class-rooms can be occupied non-stop from 7.00 am to 7.40 pm.

3. Variations in the Length of School Week

The above models may be refined by adjusting the number of days each week that pupils attend school. In Hong Kong:

- *Single-shift* schools have eight periods per day, Monday to Friday. They do not operate on Saturdays, so have 40 periods per week.

■ *Double-shift* schools have seven periods per day, Monday to Friday, plus six periods on alternate Saturdays. They have 76 periods every two weeks, or an average of 38 periods per week.

By using Saturday mornings, the double-shift schools provide almost the same total number of lessons. If they worked every Saturday instead of alternate Saturdays, double-shift schools could have even more lessons than single-shift schools. However, schooling on Saturday afternoons is unpopular in Hong Kong because government offices and many businesses work only in the mornings, and the afternoons are commonly set aside for family activities. Accordingly, the schools only operate on Saturday mornings. The afternoon session operates every afternoon from Monday to Friday, plus each *morning* on alternate Saturdays.

4. Different or Shared Teachers

Hong Kong primary schools have different teachers for morning and afternoon sessions. There is no shortage of teachers, and the government prohibits staff from working in both sessions because it is afraid that teachers will be tired and that quality will suffer. A similar policy is followed in Singapore, South Korea, and parts of Nigeria.

Other countries are less fortunate. Senegal for example is short of qualified teachers, and the authorities are keen for these limited human resources to be utilised as fully as possible. At least some staff themselves welcome opportunities to teach in more than one session, for they can increase their earnings through extra work.

5. One Set of Buildings for Two Levels of Education

Although classrooms in many systems accommodate e.g. one Grade 1 class in the morning and another Grade 1 class in the afternoon, this arrangement is not universal. In Bangladesh, for example, many double-shift primary schools teach Grades 1 and 2 in the morning and Grades 3, 4 and 5 in the afternoon.

The authorities in Puerto Rico have taken this idea even further. Some institutions accommodate elementary children in the morning and intermediate children in the afternoon. Other institutions accommodate intermediate children in the morning and high school children in the afternoon. Similar patterns are found in Palestine and India.

6. Urban and Rural Systems

Double-shift systems are most common in urban areas. This is because:

- Land is more expensive in towns. Administrators therefore try to use buildings and playgrounds as efficiently as possible.
- Urban areas have high population densities. This makes it easy to find enough pupils to run extra shifts.

But double-shift systems may also be useful in rural areas:

- Although land is less expensive, it is still important to minimise school costs.
- Rural areas often suffer from teacher shortages. Systems in which staff teach more than one set of pupils can alleviate such shortages.

Only in the smallest villages is it impossible to find enough children for a double shift. Indeed, shift schools can operate with only one teacher. The teacher takes one group of children in the morning and another in the afternoon. This type of school may be found in remote parts of India and Botswana, for example.

7. Day and Boarding Schools

Most double-shift schools are day institutions. The main objective of the double-shift system is to reduce costs, and the policy seems to go hand-in-hand with elimination of boarding in order to reduce costs further.

Although most double-shift schools are large, urban institutions, some are small and rural. The smallest type of double-shift school has only one teacher. The teacher takes one group of pupils in the morning and the other in the afternoon.

However, the two policies do not necessarily go together. Governments may find that they have to retain boarding schools in order to serve children from remote areas, but can still run the schools on a double-shift system. The schools cannot make savings on dormitories (unless they require some children to sleep at night and others to sleep in the day!), but they can make more intensive of classrooms, laboratories, kitchens, football pitches, etc.. Boarding schools can organise timetables in a more flexible way because they are not constrained by the need for children to travel early to school or to be home by nightfall. Sarawak State of Malaysia is one region which has constructed double-shift boarding schools.

8.   Daily, Weekly and Monthly Rotation

Instead of alternating in mornings and afternoons, classes may alternate by day, week or month.

- *Daily rotation*: One group of pupils attends school on Mondays, Wednesdays and Fridays while another attends on Tuesdays, Thursdays and Saturdays.
- *Weekly rotation*: One group of pupils attends school in Weeks 1 and 3, while another group attends in Weeks 2 and 4.
- *Monthly rotation*: One group of pupils attends school in January, March, May, etc., while another group attends in February, April, June, etc..

Variations of these models have been tried in several countries. They are uncommon, however, so have been excluded from the main focus of this book. They require radical reform of the education system and strong political will.

9.   Classes for both Children and Adults

Schools may be used for children in the day-time and adults in the evening. The evening classes may be taught by school teachers or by outsiders. This model is common in both industrialised and less developed countries, and is a form of double-shift system. However, this book mainly focuses on provision for school-aged children. The model is only mentioned here in order to present a complete range.

10. Borrowed and Rented Premises

In some countries, private and community schools borrow or rent the premises of public schools when the public schools close for the day. This in effect becomes a double-shift system, for the buildings are used twice by two sets of pupils.

Two illustrations may be taken from Botswana and the Philippines. In both cases, public pressure for education has led to the establishment of self-help secondary schools. The institutions are called Community Junior Secondary Schools in Botswana, and Barangay High Schools in the Philippines. In many cases the self-help institutions started life by using primary school buildings and teachers after the primary schools had closed for the day. For most institutions this was a short-term measure, but while it lasted was a form of double-shift system. Comparable institutions have existed in Pakistan and Tanzania.

In many countries, school facilities are also used for supplementary private tutoring. In some cases the tutoring is given by mainstream teachers who are already employed in the schools; but in other cases external personnel rent the classrooms for supplementary classes.

Chapter 2

Concepts of Cost Analysis

The title of this book refers to cost-effectiveness. Planners use cost-effectiveness analysis to distinguish projects which are merely cheap from ones which give good value. The term has been used in the title because it is common in everyday vocabulary. Planners may also use a related tool called cost-utility analysis. This term was not included in the title because it is less common and requires special explanation. Such explanation is among the tasks of this chapter.

Detailed examination of techniques of cost analysis reveals complexities which may not be apparent at first sight. Readers who wish to study the subject in depth are recommended to begin with the publications by Levin, Tsang and Windham noted in the 'further reading' section.

In the context of this book, however, detailed discussion is neither necessary nor possible. Accordingly this chapter is restricted to an outline of the concepts and procedures of cost analysis. It begins by highlighting three main types.

1. Three Types of Cost Analysis

Planners commonly use three different types of cost analysis.

- *Cost-benefit analysis* is used when both costs and benefits can be expressed in monetary form. It is particularly useful in industry and commerce. For example, planners may match the costs of running a proposed factory with the expected value of its produce. After making a similar calculation for a different proposed factory, the planners can compare the proposals to see which is better.

  In education, however, it is rarely possible to use cost-benefit analysis. This is because it is difficult to determine the monetary value of literacy, mathematics achievement, sporting skills, etc.. It is fairly easy for planners to calculate the costs of two schools, but it is difficult to make a monetary estimate of the products of schools.

- *Cost-effectiveness analysis* only requires the costs to be calculated in monetary terms. Effectiveness still has to be quantified, but it can be in any unit. In education, examination scores are a common measure of effectiveness.

- *Cost-utility analysis* provides a way to deal with subjective factors. The tool is especially useful in education because different people place different values on the products of education. The word 'utility' means 'usefulness'. Planners may conduct surveys to find out the utility people place on academic achievements (i.e. the extent to which those people think that academic achievement is useful or valuable). The figures for utility of academic achievement may then be contrasted with the figures for sporting and other types of achievement. Cost-utility analysis allows planners to see how well an education system is producing the sorts of products that societies want.

In education, cost-benefit analysis is used to calculate rates of return, e.g. comparing the benefits at the macro-level from investment in primary compared with secondary education. This is different in focus from the present task, however, and it will not be discussed further. Instead, the following paragraphs elaborate on the meanings of cost-effectiveness and cost-utility analysis.

2. Cost-Effectiveness Analysis: A Simple Example

The nature of cost-effectiveness analysis may best be explained through a simple example. This one is concerned with achievement: educational administrators want to raise the mathematics scores of a group of pupils. The example is fictitious, but illustrates the basic principles. In this example, the administrators assess cost-effectiveness in six steps.

Step 1: Identify Alternative Ways to Achieve the Goal

Suppose that the administrators identify four alternatives:

   i)   split mathematics classes in half, so that pupils gain more individual attention;
   ii) introduce computers on which students can practise problem-solving;
   iii) provide a special in-service training course for teachers; and

iv) prepare new and better textbooks;

Step 2: Check on the Feasibility of the Alternatives

It is useless to proceed further if the options are not actually feasible. Therefore, the policy-makers must check:

- that schools have sufficient land to build extra classrooms if they are needed to accommodate split classes, and that sufficient extra teachers are available;
- that computers can be purchased and operated as necessary;
- that appropriate instructors can be found for in-service training, and that teachers can be released to attend the courses; and
- that well-qualified authors are available to prepare new textbooks, and that facilities can be found to print and distribute the books.

It is decided in this case that all options are feasible, so none is discarded.

Step 3: Calculate the Costs of Each Strategy

i) The first method would have a high cost. Some schools would require extra new classrooms, and the authorities would have to employ more teachers. The cost is estimated at $200 per student.

ii) The second method would require special rooms, computers and some special materials, and would cost $100 per student.

iii) The third method requires teacher-trainers, facilities for training, and travelling expenses for the teachers. It would cost $60 per pupil.

iv) The fourth method would require specialist authors and printing and distribution facilities. However, unit costs would be much lower. At $30 per pupil, this method is the cheapest.

Step 4: Estimate the Effectiveness of Each Strategy

The effectiveness of each strategy can be determined by comparing the test scores of students who will gain help with those of similar students who will receive no help. On the basis of research studies and their own experience, the authorities estimate that:

i) the first method is expected to improve each pupil's score by 8 points,

ii)   the second method is expected to improve each pupil's score by 20 points,

iii) the third method is expected to improve each pupil's score by 6 points, and

iv)   the fourth method is expected to improve each pupil's score by 5 points.

Step 5: Combine the Information in a Table

This has been done in Table 1, below.

Table 1: Cost-Effectiveness of Alternative Ways to Increase Student Achievement

	Cost per (a) student	Effectiveness (test score) (b)	Cost-effectiveness (a) ÷ (b)
Split Classes	$200	8 points	$25 per point
Computers	$100	20 points	$5 per point
Teacher-Training	$60	6 points	$10 per point
Textbooks	$30	5 points	$6 per point

Step 6: Analyse the Results

From the table, two main points emerge:

■   In this example, computers are the most cost-effective innovation. It is estimated that they will cost only $5 to increase a pupil's score by one point, compared with $6 for textbooks, $10 for teacher-training, and $25 for split classes.

■   The most cost-effective strategy is not the cheapest. Textbooks would have been the cheapest, but they were only expected to raise achievement by 5 points per pupil, compared with 20 points for computers. As it happens, the most expensive strategy (split classes) was also the least cost-effective.

However, before proceeding further, policy-makers would have to check several points:

■   Although the third column of the table appears to indicate the number of dollars required for a one-point improvement in test score, it assumes that monetary investment and educational improvement are proportional. In practice, policy-makers might be faced by an 'all or none' situation. Thus, logistic factors might require them invest a full $100 per student in computers, thereby gaining a 20 point increase in effectiveness. The computers could not be broken into pieces in order to invest only $5 per student and gain a single point increase.

- In turn this implies that the authorities would need to consider the amount of money that they have available. Sometimes the budget is restricted, and expensive strategies cannot be adopted even if they are highly cost-effective.

- The example assumes that only a small group of pupils is involved. If the policy-makers wanted more widespread change, they would have to decide whether the most cost-effective option would always have the same impact, or whether the impact would diminish with scale. On the question of feasibility, the policy-makers would also have to check resource availability for large-scale implementation. If they foresaw diminishing returns and/or feasibility constraints, they might decide on a different option or on a combination of strategies.

- Most important of all, the policy-makers would have to check both that their original estimates of cost and effectiveness were reasonably accurate, and that the future would not bring major changes. A change in costs, for example, could radically change the conclusions about the most desirable investment strategy.

Box 4: Cost-Effectiveness and Cheapness

Cost-effectiveness is not necessarily the same as cheapness: some strategies may be cheap but ineffective. Sometimes it is worth investing *more* money on a project, choosing a higher-cost strategy because it also has higher effectiveness.

---

3. Cost-Utility Analysis: A Simple Example

Further complications arise when policy-makers have to consider subjective judgements on the value of outcomes. The example given above was fairly simple because it restricted analysis to a single objective: achievement scores in mathematics. However, in reality the policy-makers might have the choice e.g. of investing (i) in mathematics instruction, (ii) in reading, or (iii) a combination of mathematics and reading. In this case they would have to decide which option is most desirable; and to do this, they would have to use personal judgements.

For this type of decision, policy-makers would have to use cost-utility analysis. At least in theory, it is possible to conduct surveys to determine the utility (value) that different people place on different things. Researchers can introduce weightings if they consider the opinions of some people to be more important than the opinions of others. The researchers can then determine an 'average utility' for the item in question. Table 2 shows an example of the ways that utility and cost could be combined.

Table 2: A Hypothetical Illustration of Cost-Utility Analysis

	Instructional Strategy	
	A	B
Probability of raising mathematics performance by grade-level equivalent	.5	.3
Probability of raising reading performance by grade-level equivalent	.5	.8
Utility of raising mathematics performance by grade-level equivalent	6	6
Utility of raising reading performance by grade-level equivalent	9	9
Expected utility	$[(.5)(6)]+[(.5)(9)]$ $=7.5$	$[(.3)(6)]+[(.8)(9)]$ $=9$
Cost	$375	$400

In reality, of course, it is very difficult to make such calculations. They require a lot of data and expertise, and rest on many controversial assumptions. Sometimes, moreover, the surveys would be so expensive that the authorities would have no money left for the innovation! In practice, therefore, it is very rare for policy-makers to make precise mathematical calculations as envisaged by the theory.

Nevertheless, the basic concept remains very important. For the present context it stresses that some educational outcomes may be valued by society more highly than others, and that policy making should take this into account. Even if they cannot draw up numerical equations, policy-makers can at least list the various factors and make a general assessment of their implications and importance.

4. Cost Analysis and Multiple-Shift Schooling

It is now necessary to turn from general principles to the specific context of multiple-shift schooling. This section considers first cost-effectiveness analysis and then cost-utility analysis.

If restricting the focus to cost-effectiveness, policy-makers concerned with multiple-shift schooling would begin with identifying an objective. Suppose, for example, that the authorities want to increase school enrolments. The options might include:

- expand existing schools by opening more classes at each level,
- expand existing schools by increasing class size,
- expand existing schools by introducing double shifts, and
- build new schools.

The authorities would assess the feasibility, costs and effectiveness of each option, and would draw up policies to stress either a single strategy or a combination of strategies.

Alternatively, policy-makers might have already decided that they wished to introduce multiple shifts, but might be uncertain which model would be most appropriate. In this case they would perform the same type of analysis to compare:

- end-on double-session schooling,
- end-on triple-session schooling,
- overlapping double-session schooling,
- overlapping triple-session schooling, etc..

By itself, however, this type of analysis would probably be inadequate. In practice, decision-making often requires choice between different 'baskets' of outcomes. Thus, one strategy might have a good impact on enrolments but a bad impact on quality and on equity, while another strategy might have a less impressive impact on enrolments but cause fewer problems of quality and equity. In this case, decision-making would require some form of cost-utility analysis, assessing the importance of each outcome in a multi-dimensional way.

This, of course, is easier said than done. As noted above, policy-makers in the real world are short of information, time and technical expertise. It is unrealistic even in advanced countries to expect this type of sophisticated analysis except in very unusual circumstances.

However, even in poor countries policy-makers can still apply the principles of cost-effectiveness and cost-utility analysis in a general way. The most important point is that policies should be based on balanced and systematic assessment of:

- costs,
- effects, and
- utilities.

Policy-makers can start by listing the factors in each category, quantifying them where possible, and noting which ones are of particular importance. In the absence of full mathematical guides and research evidence, the final decision will rest on the judgement of the decision makers. At least, however, one should aim for such careful judgement, to reduce the arbitrariness of much existing policy making. The economic, educational and social ingredients for decision-making on multiple-shift schooling are discussed in Part II of this book.

PART II

DETERMINING POLICIES

Chapter 3

Economic Factors

Double-shift systems can help achieve important economic goals. They usu-ally reduce the unit costs of education, and can release both pupils and teachers for productive work elsewhere in the economy. The first part of this chapter comments on the nature and extent of these economic benefits.

However, double-shift systems may also have economic costs. They may require parents to employ people to look after children who would otherwise have been in school, and they may contribute to social problems that have economic consequences. These costs are discussed in the second part of the chapter. In most countries the benefits exceed the costs, but it is important for policy-makers to assess both sides.

1. The Economic Benefits of Double-Shift Systems

(a) Buildings and Other Facilities
Double-shift systems permit major savings in land, buildings, equipment, libraries and other facilities. A double-shift system allows two groups of pupils to use one set of facilities; and a triple-shift system allows three groups of pupils to use one set of facilities.

The savings from multiple-shift systems are often dramatic. Box 5 gives an example from Zambia in which extensive use of double and triple sessions enabled cost estimates to be reduced by 46 per cent. Maximum efficiency has been achieved by treating Grades 1-4 and Grades 5-7 sepa-rately. Grades 1-4 only have three and a half hours of classroom instruc-tion each day, so if necessary can operate in triple sessions. Grades 5-7 have five hours of classroom instruction each day, so are better retained in double sessions.

Box 5: Expansion of Education in Zambia – Alternative Cost Projections

The Government of Zambia is keen to achieve universal primary education, but is acutely conscious of resource constraints. In order to find alternative ways to reach the goal, a specially-appointed team considered use of multiple shifts.

It was obvious to the team that the nation could not afford single-session schools throughout the country, and the strategy was not even considered. Instead, recommendations focused on three main options, set out below. The capital costs of Option III (expressed in millions of Kwacha) were nearly half those of Option I.

	Number of Classrooms	Cost of Classrooms (K mill)	Toilets & Offices (K mill)	Total Cost (K mill)
Option I:	13,400	335	73	408
Grades 1–4:				
double session, rural				
triple session, urban				
Grades 5–7:				
single session, rural				
double session, urban				
Option II:	10,600	264	44	308
Grades 1–4:				
double session, rural				
double session, urban				
Grades 5–7:				
double session, rural				
double session, urban				
Option III:	8,100	202	19	221
Grades 1–4:				
double session, rural				
triple session, urban				
Grades 5–7:				
double session, rural				
double session, urban				

In Zambia, these arrangements have been implemented as long-term measures. The government is faced by ongoing growth of population, and envisages continued pressure on the education budget. In other contexts, multiple-shift schooling may also help cope with fluctuations in population and/or financial resources.

Such fluctuations, of course, are not a feature only of poor countries. Referring to the USA, one researcher has noted:

In areas of rapid growth, where new subdivisions and other housing are developed and sold, where the area is desirable and becomes stable, the number of school age children reaches a peak in a few years after the area is filled. This peak school age population continues for a number of years, even up to 20 years, but eventually it begins to drop. This drop is not as rapid as the original increase, but can eventually represent up to a 50 per cent decrease from the peak population.

School districts have tended to meet this increasing number of school age children by constructing school buildings in a sufficient number and size to accommodate the peak enrollments. As a result, long before the buildings are worn out school enrollments drop to a point where some of the schools are no longer needed. (Merrell 1980, p.2)

The writer recommended education authorities to investigate double-session schooling and other strategies to avoid this problem. As he pointed out, "overbuilding to meet peak enrollments becomes an expensive course".

However, introduction of double sessions does not always reduce costs by exactly half. This is for five reasons:

i) Extra use of facilities increases wear and tear. This creates higher maintenance costs, and in many cases requires earlier replacement or reconstruction of facilities.

ii) Schools moving to double-shift operation commonly need extra cupboards, storerooms and offices. They may also have extra study rooms or other facilities for the afternoon pupils who come early and for the morning pupils who stay late.

iii) Some governments in tropical countries also have special architectural designs for double-shift schools. Their classrooms are specially designed to withstand the afternoon heat, and are more expensive.

iv) Double-shift schools may have to be cleaned very early in the morning or very late at night. In some societies, cleaners have to be paid extra when they have to work during "unsocial" hours.

v) The fact that a system has two shifts does not always imply that it has twice the number of pupils as a single-shift system. Because the afternoon shift is usually considered less desirable than the morning one, administrators often fill up the morning shift first and only then put the 'overflow' in the afternoon shift. Introduction of double shifts only reduces costs by the proportion in the second shift.

Taking these factors into account in Jamaica, one study calculated that double-shift schooling permitted only a 32 per cent saving in buildings and facilities. Another study in Malaysia calculated only a 25 per cent saving. In both cases savings were substantial, but they were not as high as many people had initially assumed they would be. The estimates are much lower than the 46 per cent calculated for Zambia.

Box 6: Potential Economic Savings – A Missed Opportunity

Double-shift schools can reduce costs by sharing equipment and other items as well as buildings, and by making joint orders for supplies. Yet some schools fail to use this opportunity. Commenting from Nigeria, for example, one author has pointed out that each shift:

> has its own equipment carefully locked up in its own cupboard after school. The morning session headteacher and his staff have no access to the materials and documents of the afternoon session staff. Two sets of circulars are sent to each school, and even though the headteachers occupy the same offices they have different files.

The problem is especially common when separate shifts have separate headteachers, independently accountable to headquarters. Obstacles to sharing are reduced when schools have single headteachers for both sessions. But a more imaginative approach by the authorities could encour-age sharing even within schools which have separate headteachers for each session.

(b) Salaries

(i) Teachers

The extent of savings on teachers' salaries depends on the nature of the shift system. In Hong Kong and Singapore, for example, teachers are forbidden to work in both sessions. Each shift requires a full set of teachers, and the government achieves no saving in teachers' salaries.

In other systems, teachers are permitted and encouraged to work in both sessions. If teachers are paid double salary for double work, then there is no saving in salaries. However, the system does reduce the total number of teachers, which in turn reduces (i) expenditure on teachers' houses (where employing agencies are required to provide teachers' accommodation), and (ii) expenditure on teacher training.

Alternatively, teachers may receive extra pay for extra work, but at a lower rate. In Senegal, teachers who work in both shifts are paid an additional 25 per cent of their base salaries. Their work is not double that of their counterparts in single-shift schools, for double-shift schools provide only 20 hours of classroom teaching each week instead of 28 (though the school year is extended by 10 days). However, the increase in salary is a smaller proportion than the increase in work, so represents a saving for the government.

In Zambia, this type of arrangement has been made even more sophisticated through separate treatment of junior and senior classes. Official documents note that Grades 1-4 only have three and a half hours of lesson time each day, that the normal working day lasts for eight hours, and that in theory a teacher should be able to teach two sessions each day. However, policy advisers realise that:

> a teacher who was so intensively occupied with actual classroom teaching would not have much time for the preparation of work, especially in situations where the shortage of formal teaching materials might necessitate much time for improvisation and seeking for alternatives.

The authorities therefore decided to limit the teacher's classroom work to about six hours a day in order to allow time for lesson preparation. This meant that two teachers would be sufficient for three sessions. Even if the teachers were paid higher salaries in recognition of the extra work, it was pointed out, "the extra payments would fall far short of the salary for an additional teacher who might otherwise be required".

At the same time, the Zambian authorities recognised that differences in the workload for Grades 5-7 teachers required alternative arrangements:

> At the grade 5-7 level there is a greater need for a teacher to have time to correct pupils' written work in addition to the time required for preparing class materials. Hence it would not seem advisable to have a regular class teacher at this level heavily engaged during a second session on the same day, though if contact hours for each session are reduced to five [from five hours and 20 minutes in single sessions] he could make some contribution to the second session. A subject-teacher, on the other hand, could teach in both sessions within a regular quota of contact hours.

This analysis highlights the value of flexible policies which recognise that the workloads of different types of teacher may vary.

(ii) Clerks and Ancillary Staff

Although double-shift schools in Singapore and Puerto Rico have two teams of teachers, they have only one team of clerks, cleaners, labourers and messengers. This arrangement allows the authorities to make salary savings. Governments of other countries also make savings in the salaries of night-watchmen, for the use of double shifts means that they have fewer school compounds.

Use of a single team of ancillary staff to serve a double-session school does of course require careful management. Working hours are usually staggered to ensure that someone is on the compound at all hours of the school day.

(c) Time and Labour

When a double-shift system has a shorter day than a single-shift system, it saves the time and labour of teachers and pupils.

- If *teachers* work only in one shift, they are free for other economic activities, for study, or for domestic activities.
- *Pupils* are also released for longer periods of the day. This is especially important in societies where school-children earn a living outside school hours. The fact that pupils can both go to school *and* earn a living may allow poor children to attend school. This reduces social inequalities and raises the overall educational level of the society.

Release of pupils may also generate an alternative economic benefit. In many societies, older children are needed to look after their younger brothers and sisters while their parents go to work. Pupils in double-shift schools may have more time each day to help their families in this way.

Box 7: Double-Shift Schooling and Child Labour

In many poor countries children play a crucial economic role, trading and caring for children younger than themselves. It is not unusual to even find morning-shift *teachers* immediately going to their businesses or homes when classes finish, to release young people for the afternoon shift at school.

In the absence of the shift system, either the teachers would be prevented from teaching because they could not leave the businesses or families; or the children would not be able to attend school at all. The shift system allows everybody to get the best of both worlds.

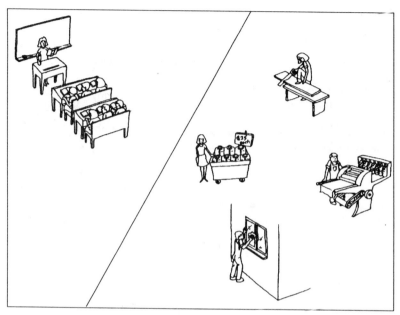

*Double-shift schooling can release young people for productive work in the economy.
They may attend school in the morning and then work in the afternoon (or vice versa).*

2. The Economic Costs of Double-Shift Systems

In some systems, the benefits noted in the previous section must be set
against certain economic costs before a final balance sheet can be pro-
duced. Three costs are worth particular mention.

(a) Child-Minding Agencies

In addition to their educational function, schools serve a child-minding
function. They keep children occupied during the day, and this allows
their parents to get on with their own work. Half-day schools do not occupy children as long as full-day schools. In some societies this requires parents to send their children either to relatives or to special child-minding
agencies and playgroups.

Box 8: Double-Shift Schooling and the Extra Costs of Child-Minding

Double-shift systems can create problems for working parents. Children either start and finish school early, or start and finish school late. School hours do not match working hours, and children cannot spend extra time in school because facilities are constantly in use by other shifts.

Some working parents solve this problem by asking grandmothers or other relatives to look after their children, but others have to employ child-minding agencies. In the latter case, shift schooling saves money for the government but increases costs for the parents. The savings for society as a whole are less than they appear at first sight.

In Hong Kong, for example, community groups and commercial enterprises rent or construct buildings where children can do their homework and be supervised. In many cases, they also employ staff to organise educational activities and games. Informal estimates suggest that about 10% of primary school children go to such centres on a regular basis.

(b) Tutors

When a double-shift system seriously reduces the length of a school day, parents often become concerned about the extent to which their children are able to cover the curriculum. Centres of the type mentioned above often have an educational as well as a child-minding function. Parents may find that they need to send their children to such centres or to private tutors just for the educational benefits, even if they do not need the child-minding services. Tutorial classes are often expensive because they are small and are run as profit-making enterprises.

One particularly serious situation has been reported in Lebanon, where many teachers offer extra tutorial lessons outside class hours. In some cases, teachers have refused to teach properly during school hours because they know that they can make extra money by teaching the same pupils after school. This could happen in a single-session system, but the problem is exacerbated in a double-session system because the teachers argue that there is no time to cover the full curriculum during normal school hours. This type of abuse obviously requires careful monitoring. One safeguard used for example in Singapore and the Republic of Korea is to prohibit teachers from organising paid tutorials for their own school pupils.

(c) Social Welfare Costs

It was mentioned above that double-shift systems can release young people for productive employment. However, in some societies it is very hard for such youths to find jobs. Instead of finding work, they join gangs and exacerbate social problems. Although the government may save money through a double-shift system, it may have to spend money to deal with social problems. It is usually difficult to make precise estimates of the extra expenditure required, but the question should not be ignored.

3. Summary

Double-shift systems can provide major economic benefits. They are:

- more efficient use of buildings and other facilities,
- more efficient use of scarce teachers (if staff are allowed to teach in more than one session),
- savings in teacher training and teacher housing (if the shift system allows reduction in the total number of teachers),
- release of teachers for other work in the economy (if the system reduces the number of classroom hours in each shift and if the teachers decide to take on other work), and
- release of pupils for productive work in the economy.

These benefits must be set against some potential costs before the final balance can be assessed. The chief costs are:

- the need for working parents to employ child-minding agencies,
- the potential need for extra tuition to compensate for reduced classroom time, and
- the costs for social welfare if out-of-school youth create extra social problems because they have more idle time.

Even after allowance for these costs, however, in almost all cases the final balance sheet is strongly positive. Double-shift schooling can provide major economic benefits.

Chapter 4
Educational Factors

The economic benefits discussed in the previous chapter must be balanced against various educational costs. This chapter has four main parts. It focuses in turn on the general atmosphere of double-shift schools, on cognitive achievement, on curriculum duration and content, and on extra-curricular activities.

1. The General Atmosphere of Double-Shift Schools

Most educators agree that the atmosphere of double-shift schools is inferior to that of single-shift schools. In double-shift systems:

- The school day is more pressurised. Everybody always seems to be in a hurry. Breaks are shortened, and teaching-time is sometimes reduced.
- Pupils and staff of different shifts do not easily identify with each other. In a double-shift system they feel like two schools, not one. This is especially true when each shift has a separate headteacher.
- When morning classes begin very early, children sometimes miss their breakfast. They later become hungry and find it difficult to concentrate on lessons.
- Especially in hot climates, children find it hard to study in the afternoons because they are tired. Teachers are also tired in the afternoons, particularly if they have already taught full morning sessions.
- Teachers who work in more than one session may have less time to prepare classes and to correct assignments.
- The large student population makes it difficult for the staff to know all students personally, and can exacerbate discipline problems. Pupils may stay on the school compound but evade classes, pre-tending that they are members of the out-of-lessons shift.
- If afternoon-shift pupils come to school early, they may be noisy and may disturb the lessons of the morning-shift pupils. Similar problems arise if the morning-shift pupils stay late instead of going home as soon as their classes are finished.

- On the other hand, if afternoon-shift pupils are prohibited from arriving until it is time for their lessons, and if all the morning-shift children leave school as soon as classes are over, then the transition period may be chaotic. The sudden emptying and refilling of the school reduces the children's and teachers' sense of belonging. It makes the school seem like a 'teaching machine' or factory.
- Teachers cannot use classroom wall-space so freely. The morning-shift pupils may tamper with the wall pictures of the afternoon-shift pupils, and vice versa. Likewise, teachers cannot leave work on the blackboard overnight. Pupils and teachers have less sense of ownership of their classrooms.
- The following sections of this chapter show that these problems do not necessarily have a disastrous impact on pupils' learning. However, policy-makers should at least be aware of these reasons why double-shift schooling is so widely disliked.

Afternoons may be particularly problematic in double-shift schools. Both teachers and pupils are tired.

**Box 9: Contrasting Double-Session and Single-Session Schools –
Observations from Singapore**

An official report by the Singapore Ministry of Education compared learning conditions in double-session and single-session schools. It noted two major problems
in double-session schools:

- It was difficult to arrange either remedial or enrichment classes, because
  classrooms were often not available outside the hours for each session.
- Most double-session schools operated as two separate institutions in the
  same compound. Rarely did all staff and pupils come together at the same
  time, and it was difficult to build cohesive and distinctive school communities.

Single-session schools, in contrast, were planned and co-ordinated more effectively. Relationships between teachers and pupils were also better because people
stayed back more often for formal and informal activities. A greater sense of
belonging made school life more enriching and enjoyable.

These observations match the experience of educators in other countries. By
themselves they do not necessarily imply that double-session schools should be
abolished, for the educational costs might be outweighed by the economic and
other benefits. However, they do highlight some important contrasts between
double-session and single-session schooling.

---

2. Double-Shift Schooling and Cognitive Achievement

The observations about the general atmosphere of double-shift schools
would at first sight seem very serious. However, in practice this is not
always so.

Reliable research evidence which compares cognitive achievement in
different types of system is difficult to find. One reason is that individual
schools cannot easily be compared. In countries with more than one type
of system, single-session schools are commonly:

- remote schools with populations too low to justify more than one
  shift,
- unpopular schools which would have double sessions if there was
  enough demand but do not actually have enough pupils, or
- elite schools which have lots of money so are not anxious to minimise unit costs.

In contrast, double-session schools are usually urban, are reasonably popular, and serve poor or middle-income families. When academic achieve-

ment between schools varies, it is often because of these other factors rather than because of the number of shifts.

Nevertheless, some research findings are worth summarising.

1. *Brazil*: Fuller et al. (1999) studied determinants of literacy in urban and rural primary schools in Northeast Brazil. They tested Grade 1 and 2 children in 140 schools in two provinces. Most of the urban schools operated either two or three shifts. The researchers found "no evidence that multiple shifts in schools are negatively associated with early literacy levels". They noted that if multiple shifts lead to serious denigration of facilities, then parental support for schools may decline; but, they added, "if schools are reasonably maintained, it does not appear that multiple shifts yield negative achievement effects".

2. *Chile*: Many schools have operated with double sessions, and some have had triple sessions. Farrell & Schiefelbein (1974) surveyed 353 Grade 8 classes, collecting data from 10 students in each class and from all teachers and school directors. They concluded that "there is almost no association between level of academic performance and the number of shifts in which a school is utilized daily".

3. *India*: Batra (1998) compared scores of Class IV students in 23 schools in Assam and Madhya Pradesh. In Assam, double-shift students scored marginally better than single-shift students in mathematics, but not so well in other subjects. In Madhya Pradesh, double-shift students scored marginally higher in science and social science, but not so well in language or mathematics. Overall, Batra concluded, "it appears that the double-shift schools are not necessarily achieving any better educational results or performing any worse than the students of single-shift schools".

4. *Malaysia*: Beebout (1972) examined the academic achievement of 7,674 senior secondary students in 89 West Malaysian schools. Some of the schools were Malay-medium, while others were English-medium. Among the Malay-medium schools the researcher found that academic scores were higher in single-session institutions. Among the English-medium schools, however, the performance of double-session pupils was as good as the single-session pupils.

   Beebout further noted that schools which were purpose-built for double sessions had classrooms which were specially designed to cope with the afternoon heat, and had extra rooms for use by afternoon students who arrived early (or by morning students who stayed late). He observed that where negative achievement had occurred, it was:

> thought to be partly due to the fact that present double-session schools were originally designed as single-session schools. Problems of student congestion and afternoon heat are more severe than if facilities were designed for double sessions.

5. *Nigeria:* Emeka Anyanwu studied First School Leaving Certificate examination scores in Imo State, and found lower pass rates among double-shift schools. His finding partly reflected the low socio-economic status of many double-shift pupils, for the afternoon sessions chiefly enrol domestic servants and similar low-status people. Anyanwu also noted that double-shift schools still had much larger classes than most single-shift schools. Yet even after allowance for these facts it appeared that performance in double-shift schools might still be inferior. Anyanwu observed that "teachers and pupils are always tense because of the nature of the timetable and the reduced recreation period".

6. *Senegal:* In 1982 the Ministry of Education launched a pilot double-session system at the primary level. Seven years later, evaluators of the project reported that:

> the results of student performance in the classrooms experimenting with the double-shift system, compared to the results of regular classrooms, was positive; student scores in tested areas (reading, writing, math) were generally higher. Hence, it was concluded that reduction of the teaching time did not have adverse consequences on student learning levels, perhaps due in part to the lower student/teacher ratio.

Following this evaluation, the programme was considerably expanded.

Although these findings are not entirely consistent, their overall tone is positive. The studies suggest that the academic achievement of children in double-shift systems is often just as high as that of children in single-shift systems. Two points in favour of double shifts are worth particular stress:

■ introduction of double shifts may permit reduction in class size and therefore a more personalised teaching approach, and

■ double-shift schools are generally larger, and therefore find it easier to justify expenditure on libraries, laboratories, etc..

Indeed if these two factors weigh heavily enough, introduction of double shifts can actually *improve* quality.

3. Curriculum Duration and Content

The duration of teaching-time in double-shift systems has already been mentioned, but deserves further attention. The content of curricula also requires discussion.

Table 3 shows official data on primary school teaching-time in 13 countries. In seven countries, teaching-time has been shortened to accommodate extra shifts. However, in six countries no reduction has been made.

Similar analysis of the secondary level would probably reveal a larger proportion of systems which have fewer hours in double-shift compared with single-shift systems. Most secondary school systems require six to seven hours of teaching per day, and it is much more difficult to operate double shifts without cutting this length of time. Nevertheless, the fact that a significant number of systems have not reduced the hours at the primary level is important.

Another feature reflected in the table, applicable to both primary and secondary levels, concerns the duration of official classroom teaching-time, of which the table shows wide variation. For example, according to the table, Ghanaian single-session primary classes all have 22 hours and 55 minutes of classroom instruction per week. This contrasts with Burkina Faso where single-session schools have 30 hours. Information on the number of weeks of term-time each year might show that the variations are smaller than the table implies, but it is unlikely that differences would be cancelled altogether.

A further point emerging from the table is that even the shortened double-shift allocation is longer in some countries than the full single-shift allocation of other countries. For instance, the 24 hours 10 minutes of the Philippines' double-shift senior primary schools is longer than the full single shifts of Ghana, Hong Kong, Laos and Nigeria. This implies that when classroom time is reduced because of the introduction of a shift system, the impact may not be disastrous. Much depends on the length of curriculum time before the change.

Table 3: Official Weekly Classroom-Instruction Time (Primary Schools)

		Single Session	Double Session	Triple Session
Burkina Faso		30h 00m	21h 00m	–
The Gambia		26h 00m	23h 45m	–
Ghana		22h 55m	19h 35m	–
Hong Kong		23h 20m	22h 10m	–
Jamaica		25h 00m	22h 30m	–
Laos	(junior)	19h 00m	19h 00m	–
	(senior)	22h 00m	22h 00m	–
Malaysia	(junior)	22h 30m	22h 30m	–
	(senior)	24h 00m	24h 00m	–
Myanmar		25h 00m	25h 00m	–
Nigeria, Imo State		22h 05m	22h 05m	–
Philippines	(junior)	25h 00m	23h 20m	–
	(senior)	30h 00m	24h 10m	–
Senegal		28h 00m	20h 00m*	–
Singapore	(junior)	22h 30m	22h 30m	–
	(senior)	24h 30m	24h 30m	–
Zambia	(junior)	20h 25m	20h 25m	17h 30m
	(senior)	26h 40m	26h 40m	–

*But with a school year extended by 10 days.
Note: These are officially recommended periods of teaching. Many governments permit institutions to make some variation. Also, periodic reforms may change the official numbers of hours.

Turning to the actual content of the curriculum, it should first be noted that the research studies cited above tend to be biased. When teaching time is shortened, the first casualties are usually such subjects as music, handicraft, moral guidance, and religion. The bulk of research work uses narrow criteria for academic achievement, often focusing only on language, mathematics, science and a few other academic subjects. When the curriculum is shortened following the introduction of a shift system, these may be the subjects that are retained, and so one should expect achievement in them to remain high. The real curriculum losses of double-shift systems may be in the other areas.

Secondly, it is obvious that good teachers who are well supported with curriculum resources and materials can achieve a great deal more in a short time than bad teachers with few materials can achieve in twice the time. This point stresses the need for authorities to note ways to maintain or improve quality, highlighted in Chapter 8 of this book.

4. Double-Shift Schooling and Extra-Curricular Activities

Achievement in classroom subjects is of course not the only goal of school life. Education systems also aim to promote healthy attitudes and physical development. Extra-curricular activities provide one of the main ways to achieve these goals. Through sporting activities, children learn about cooperation and competition as well as how to grow physically strong and healthy. They develop other talents in music, drama, debating, chess, scouting, and so on.

It is generally said that shift schooling forces authorities to cut back on extra-curricular activities. The school day becomes too tight, and compounds may be too congested to allow simultaneous activity by children of all sessions. Schools with large compounds may find that they can allow afternoon-session pupils to come early to practise gymnastics, to play basketball, to join a school choir, or to rehearse the school play; but schools with small compounds find first that there is simply not enough space, and second that the noise from the ball games and music groups disturbs the children who are studying.

Further difficulties arise in the organisation of inter-school sports competitions. When most schools have only single shifts, competitions are commonly held on weekday afternoons. Schools with double shifts then find that:

- all the sports players have to be enrolled in the morning session (thereby creating an imbalance), or
- sports players in afternoon sessions have to miss classes from time to time, or
- sports players in afternoon sessions have to be excluded from inter-school competitions.

However, there may be ways to get round problems of this type. One solution is to hold inter-school competitions on Saturday mornings. An alternative solution is to hold two types of competition: one for single-shift schools, and one for double-shift schools. Chapter 8 of this book highlights similar ways through which other problems may at least be reduced.

Finally, one point raised in connection with academic achievement also applies to extra-curricular activities. Schools with large populations find it easier to justify investment in swimming pools, gymnasia, sports fields, etc.. In this respect, double-shift schools may actually have an advantage over single-shift schools.

Box 10: Double Shifts and Extra-Curricular Activities

Elsa Leo-Rhynie and colleagues have evaluated Jamaica's system of double-session schooling. One of their questions was whether schools had had to stop extra-curricular activities in order to accommodate the extra shift. The researchers' findings were:

	No. of Schools Investigated	No. of Schools which had to Stop:		
		Clubs & Societies	Minor Games	Major Games
Primary	11	0	0	0
All Age	32	9	2	4
Grammar & Technical	8	0	0	0

Just over a quarter of the all-age schools reported that they had had to stop clubs and societies, and a few all-age schools reported that they had had to stop games. However no primary, grammar or technical schools had had the same experience.

The research suggests that while double-shift schooling may have severe implications for extra-curricular activities, it does not necessarily do so. Most Jamaican schools had found ways round the constraints imposed by double sessions.

---

5. Summary

Double-shift schools certainly may suffer educational disadvantages compared with single-shift schools. Teaching time for each shift may be reduced, and the need to compress a lot of activity into a short time may make the school day rather tense. Both children and teachers may be tired, particularly during afternoon shifts in hot countries. This may affect not only academic aspects of school life but also social and extra-curricular activities.

However, these educational costs are not always serious. Some research has indicated that academic achievement in double-shift schools may be just as high as in single-shift schools, and administrators with imagination may find ways to get round the problems both of shorter school days and of congested school compounds.

Chapter 5

Social Factors

The total balance sheet for policy-makers must take account of social as well as economic and educational factors. This chapter begins by noting the potential impact of double-shift systems on social equity. It then turns to questions of 'restless out-of-school youth'.

1. Shift Systems and Social Equity

Double-shift systems can greatly contribute to social equity, for they permit governments to increase access to education at a moderate cost. Governments may be faced by a choice between:

- single-shift schooling for some and no schooling for others, or
- double-shift schooling for everybody.

The second option is much more equitable. It may require some sacrifice of quality for pupils who would have had places in the first option, but society's resources are spread to cover more people.

Double-shift systems can also help low-income groups in other ways:

- Some families are too poor to allow members to spend the whole day in school, for they cannot afford to lose the income that children and youths could gain from working. Systems of half-day schooling reduce this problem. They allow young people to attend school and still earn a living.
- Even when young people from poor families do not directly earn money, they are often needed to look after younger children. Double- shift schooling may enable young people to undertake domestic duties in turn: while one is in school, another is out of school, and vice versa.
- Poor children are also excluded from school by high fees. Double-shift schooling reduces costs, so can also reduce school fees.

Nevertheless, it is rare for everybody to attend a double-shift school.

single session

double session

triple session

A system of single-session schooling may force authorities to exclude many children from school. A double-session system permits higher enrolments and fewer rejections. From the viewpoint of equity, a triple-session system might be the best of all.

Unless policy-makers are careful, double-session schooling reinforces social inequalities. It is important to consider the equity implications of different strategies:

- *Rural versus Urban.* Rural schools are often disadvantaged by comparison with urban schools. They have less reliable supplies of books and other materials, they are less likely to have well-qualified teachers, they may have to operate multigrade classes, and in poor countries they may not have electricity or other amenities.

  On the other hand, Chapter 1 noted that rural schools are less likely to have double-shift systems. A policy which only requires urban schools to have double shifts could help compensate for other inequities in the system.

- *Rich versus Poor.* Inequities also exist within urban areas. Rich communities are usually more influential than poor ones, and may protest against their children attending double-shift schools. Double- shift systems reinforce inequalities if they are only found in poor communities. Social justice requires double-shift systems to be operated in rich communities too.

- *Different Racial Groups.* Under apartheid in colonial Zimbabwe (then called Southern Rhodesia), different education systems served the European, Asian, Coloured and Black populations. Shortly before Independence in 1980, the schools for European, Asian and Coloured populations were renamed Group A schools, and those for Blacks were renamed Group B schools. The categories were unified after Independence, but real racial integration was slow and major funding disparities persisted. Reflecting these disparities, two decades after Independence double-shift schooling was much more common in former Group B than in former Group A schools. Namibia faced a similar problem. Double-shift schooling in these two countries was perceived to perpetuate racial as well as class inequalities. It would have been preferable to have had the same system for schools serving all communities.

- *Academically Bright versus Academically Weak.* During the 1980s and 1990s, in Trinidad & Tobago only junior secondary schools (Forms 1-3) operated double shifts. Full secondary schools (Forms 1-5) had single shifts. Allocation was based on examination results: pupils with good results went to full secondary schools, and the rest went to junior secondary schools.

In such circumstances, it was hardly surprising that society associated double-shift schooling with low academic achievement; and
in so far as double shifting imposed constraints on the teachers,
junior secondary schools suffered a double handicap.

Research has shown that academic performance is not just
determined by children's inborn ability; it is also determined by
home support and learning conditions. Thus, while at first sight
the system in Trinidad & Tobago only differentiated between
bright and dull children, in practice it also differentiated between
rich and poor. Full secondary schools drew mainly from high
socio-economic groups, while junior secondary schools drew
mainly from low socio-economic groups.

If policy-makers had wished to make the system more equitable,
they would have reversed it. The full-day schools would have
either operated double shifts or selected only the low academic
achievers; and the junior secondary schools would have either
operated single shifts or selected only the high academic achievers.
However, this policy change would have been political dynamite.
It would have challenged the privileges of the rich, and would have
caused strong opposition from influential groups. It would probably have been more politically realistic simply to ensure that all
schools were either single-shift or double-shift.

■ *Desirable versus Undesirable Sessions.* Inequities may also exist within double-shift schools. Morning sessions are usually considered
more desirable than afternoon ones. It might be unfair for some
children to benefit from morning sessions for the whole of their
school careers while other children suffer from afternoon sessions
for the whole of their school careers.

This problem can be reduced through systems of internal
organisation discussed in Chapter 6. For example, if a double- session primary school has Grades 1, 3 and 5 in the morning and
Grades 2, 4 and 6 in the afternoon, then all children alternate
between morning and afternoon sessions as they progress through
the system. Alternatively, schools might have Grades 1-6 in the
morning and parallel Grades 1-6 in the afternoon, but could then
require classes to rotate from time to time.

Teachers in double-session systems also tend to prefer morning
sessions. Policy-makers should guard against the danger of good

teachers all gravitating to the morning session. This requires deliberate effort to secure even distribution of good staff. A schedule of teacher rotation like the schedule of pupil rotation might help to make the system more fair.

Box 11: How Often should Pupils Alternate between Sessions?

Double-shift systems can be made more fair if pupils alternate between different sessions. Pupils who begin with morning classes are later asked to attend afternoon classes, and vice versa.

The question is then how often the students should alternate. Every month? Every term? Every year?

The question has no fixed answer. Yearly rotation is perhaps the most simple and the least disruptive of family patterns. When classes alternate too often, parents get confused and families find it hard to settle into routines.

However some authorities advocate more frequent rotation to promote both equity and variety. Zambian double-shift schools are expected to rotate classes every term, many schools in Laos rotate classes every month, one report in Ghana has recommended classes to rotate every two weeks, and some classes in The Gambia and Zimbabwe rotate every week.

---

2. Problems of 'Restless Youth'

Chapter 3 pointed out that double-shift systems may reduce the length of a school day, which releases young people for productive work in the economy. In this case, there is an economic benefit. But in some societies school-aged children cannot find work. Either there is no work, because unemployment is too high, or labour laws prohibit employment of youths under a specified age.

In the latter cases, double-shift systems may contribute to problems of 'restless youth' and delinquency. When young people attend school for shorter periods each day, they have more time to hang around in the streets and get bored. Even if the school day is not shorter, pupils in double-session systems are free for the whole morning or the whole afternoon. In contrast to the schedule for single-session pupils, the schedule for double-session pupils does not occupy the central part of the day. This means that they have a longer stretch of time in which to get bored. Problems are increased when double-shift systems reduce contact between teachers and pupils, thereby restricting the effectiveness of school-based guidance and support.

Box 12: Double Shifts and Youth Indiscipline – Contrasting Views

The double-shift system in Jamaica has been criticised for allowing adolescent students too much free time, "which is used in carrying out acts of vandalism, drug use and illicit sex". Similar comments may be heard in many other societies, ranging from Nigeria to the India.

However, the fact that some young people get into trouble does not imply that they are all delinquent. Many young people use their free time in highly productive ways, engaging in worthwhile hobbies, earning money, and helping their families.

Authorities must therefore assess these contrasting possibilities in the context of their specific circumstances. Planners cannot assume that extra free time is always good. But nor can they assume that it is always bad.

To some extent, the accusation against the school system may be unfair: it expects schools to solve a problem which has nothing to do with education. School authorities could rightly protest against the idea that the function of schools is to keep young people off the streets.

Yet although this is not the main function of schools, it is undeniably one role that they play. Policy-makers have to weigh up the costs and benefits of:

- insisting on full-day schooling in order to keep young people occupied for longer periods and for the central part of each day (while also giving the schools sufficient resources to make the longer school day meaningful),
- retaining half-day schooling and using the resources saved for other social welfare programmes to help the young people, or
- simply neglecting the issue, implementing neither of these options.

PART III

MAKING DOUBLE-SHIFT SCHOOLS WORK

Chapter 6
School Organisation and Timetabling

Double-shift schooling requires careful organisation in order to operate efficiently and effectively. This chapter comments first on alternative arrangements of classes within double-shift schools. It then turns to details of timetabling.

1. Which Classes should be Taught in which Shifts?

Should junior classes study in the morning or the afternoon? What about the senior classes? Should classes alternate between shifts, or should pupils join one shift and stay in it permanently? These questions are addressed in this section.

(a) Primary Schools
The range of options for internal organisation may be illustrated by reference to a six-grade, double-shift primary school. Six options are considered here.

Option 1: Grades 1 to 6 in the morning, and parallel Grades 1 to 6 in the afternoon.

Advantages:
- The morning and afternoon sessions operate like two independent schools. They can have different staffs and even different head-teachers.
- Children can stay in either the morning or the afternoon shift for the whole of their school careers. This may make life easier to organise for their families. If they have brothers or sisters in the same shift, every-body can go to school and leave school together.
- Equipment and materials used e.g. by the Grade 1 class in the morning can be used by the parallel Grade 1 class in the afternoon.

Disadvantages:
- Teachers of the same grade cannot coordinate easily. The morning

teachers of Grade 3 may not see the afternoon teachers of Grade 3. This may cause problems when deciding on the furniture for classrooms, purchasing books for class libraries, setting examinations, etc..

- The morning and afternoon sessions have separate identities. They may not feel like one school.
- The afternoon session is usually less popular than the morning one. It may be difficult to attract good teachers, and the pupils and staff may feel inferior. Parents may exert pressure to get their children transferred from the afternoon to the morning session.
- The system seems unfair. Children who are allocated to the morning session have an advantage, while children allocated to the afternoon suffer a disadvantage.

Option 2: Grades 1, 2 and 3 in the morning, and Grades 4, 5 and 6 in the afternoon.

Advantages:
- During their six years at school, children study in both morning and afternoon sessions. This is more fair.
- Teachers of the same grade can easily liaise with each other.
- Children of the same age-group have more peers with whom to socialise.
- Pupils in the same grade can all sit examinations together.
- In some systems, senior classes have longer hours than junior classes. It may therefore be better to group all senior classes together and all junior classes together. Examples of curriculum times from several countries were given in Chapter 4. A more detailed example from Solomon Islands is provided in Box 13.

Disadvantages:
- Pupils in Grades 1, 2 and 3 have to use the same desks and chairs as pupils in Grades 4, 5 and 6, even though the children are physically of different sizes. Special furniture designs may be needed.
- It is necessary to buy two sets of class readers, etc., because all children of the same grade are at school together.
- In many systems, Grade 6 pupils have to take an important examination. They are in the afternoon session, and may find it hard to concentrate.
- The morning session has no pupils above Grade 3. It loses the leadership that senior pupils can provide.

Box 13: Different Periods of Study for Different Grades?

In some systems, junior children are started off gently with a shortened school day. Their ability to concentrate improves as they get older, and more is demanded from them as they progress through the school system.

In Solomon Islands the curriculum for Standards 1 and 2 has only four hours of teaching time. For Standard 3 it has four and a half hours, and for Standards 4, 5 and 6 it has five hours.

Such variation in the duration of teaching has implications for organisation of double-shift systems. It may be best for all children of the same grade to study at the same time. Thus, if all the Standard 1 and 2 children start together, they will all finish together. Standard 3 is anomalous; but if Standard 3 classes start with Standards 1 and 2, they will finish only 30 minutes later. This arrangement releases all classrooms for Standards 4, 5 and 6, and simplifies general organisation.

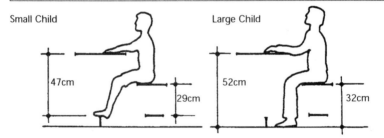

Most primary schools in Bangladesh accommodate Grades 1 and 2 in the morning and Grades 3, 4 and 5 in the afternoon. UNESCO staff have designed special furniture for use by pupils of different sizes. The table has a bar underneath which small children can use as a foot-rest; and the bench has a shelf underneath for small children to use as a foot-rest and for other children to store books.

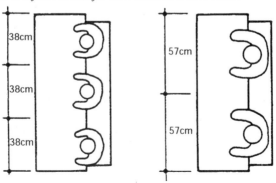

The designers also recognised that (a) many children drop out of school after the early grades and (b) large children need more horizontal space. Accordingly, they designed their furniture to accommodate either three small children or two large ones.

Option 3: Grades 4, 5 and 6 in the morning, and Grades 1, 2 and 3 in the afternoon. This is the reverse of Option 2. Most points are similar, but this option has two additional advantages and one additional disadvantage.

Advantages:
- Grade 6, the examination class, is in the morning. Pupils may find it easier to concentrate on their studies.
- Junior children start in the afternoon, and later move to the morning session. This gives them something to look forward to. Instead of feeling that they have lost a privilege, the senior children feel that they have won a privilege.

Disadvantage:
- Children who are just beginning school have to start with an afternoon session. This places an extra burden on small children at a critical point in their lives.

Option 4: Grades 1, 3 and 5 in the morning, and Grades 2, 4 and 6 in the afternoon.

Advantages:
- As children move through the school system, they alternate between morning and afternoon sessions.
- Teachers of individual grades can liaise easily.
- Grade 1 children are given the morning session.

Disadvantages:
- Alternation of morning and afternoon sessions may cause problems for families, especially if other children are in opposite sessions.
- As in Options 2 and 3, it is necessary to buy two sets of class readers, etc. because all children of the same grade are at school together.
- Grade 6 children (who may be taking important examinations) are in the afternoon session.
- Grade 6 children do not feel they have won the privilege of studying in the morning for their last year.

Option 5: Grades 2, 4 and 6 in the morning, and Grades 1, 3 and 5 in the afternoon. This is the reverse of Option 4. Similar points apply, but some are reversed.

Advantages:
- Grade 6 pupils study in the morning.
- Grade 5 pupils, who study in the afternoon, can look forward to the privilege of studying in the morning when they reach Grade 6.

Disadvantage:
- Grade 1 children have to start their school careers with afternoon study.

Option 6: Grades 1, 2, 5 and 6 in the morning, and Grades 3 and 4 in the afternoon.

Box 13 noted that in many countries junior grades have fewer hours of instruction each day than do senior grades. The box gave the specific example of Solomon Islands, suggesting that in this case it was preferable to teach Grades 1, 2 and 3 in one session, and Grades 4, 5 and 6 in the other.

Sometimes the difference in the number of hours of instruction for each grade is so great that another pattern becomes possible. In some Indonesian schools, for example, the duration of daily teaching (excluding breaks) is:

Grades 1 and 2: 2 hours and 30 minutes,
Grades 3 and 4: 4 hours and 10 minutes,
Grades 5 and 6: 4 hours and 30 minutes.

This means that two sessions of Grade 1 or 2 take only a little more time than a single session of Grade 5 or 6. In turn, this means that schools can operate as indicated in Table 4.

Table 4: Timetable for a School with Grades 1, 2, 5 and 6 in the Morning and Grades 3 and 4 in the Afternoon

	Grade Total	School Day	Break Times
Morning Session	1	8.00 – 10.40	9.30 – 9.40
	2	10.40 – 1.20	11.55 – 12.05
	5	8.00 – 1.00	10.00 – 10.15
			11.30 – 11.45
	6	8.00 – 1.00	10.00 – 10.15
			11.30 – 11.45
Afternoon Session	3	1.00 – 5.30	3.00 – 3.10
			4.30 – 4.40
	4	1.00 – 5.30	3.00 – 3.10
			4.30 – 4.40

Advantages:
- Both the children starting school for the first time and the senior children preparing for examinations have classes in the morning.
- More classes attend school in the morning than in the afternoon.

Disadvantage:
- The model is only possible in systems with very short teaching times for pupils in Grades 1 and 2. While it is common for junior grades to study for fewer hours than senior grades, the gap is not usually as wide as in shown here. Many educators would argue that daily teaching time of just 2 hours and 30 minutes is too short.

This discussion shows that school administrators may have a wide range of options. The options are not necessarily exclusive, for in many education systems some or all of the models operate side by side.

In some countries, school authorities are permitted to decide for themselves which model to use. In other countries, central authorities decide on the best system and then issue instructions to individual schools.

(b) Secondary Schools

The options for secondary schools may be broadly similar to the options for primary schools. However, some additional factors may need to be considered:

i) *Senior Classes in a '5 + 2' System.* Many countries have a '5 + 2' secondary school structure, i.e. with junior secondary school lasting for five years and leading to a school certificate, followed by senior secondary school lasting for two years and leading to a higher school certificate.

Double-session institutions may choose to have one set of Forms 1 to 5 in the morning and another set of Forms 1 to 5 in the afternoon. But they are then left with the problem of Forms 6 and 7. Teachers for these classes are often more highly qualified than the other staff. If Forms 6 and 7 are put in only one shift, then the other pupils in that shift have an advantage not shared by their colleagues.

One solution is to allow Forms 6 and 7 to operate across the shifts. Careful timetabling can allow the students to come halfway through the morning shift and to leave halfway through the after-noon shift. Schools which have tried this system have found that it is harder to supervise the Forms 6 and 7 students because they come and go at odd times. They have also found that the senior students provide less leadership because they are less involved in school life. Nevertheless, the model can be made to work reason-ably well.

ii) *Forms 1–3 versus Forms 4 & 5*. An alternative system avoids this problem by placing Forms 1–3 in one shift and Forms 4 and 5 in another. Forms 6 and 7 can then be taught with Forms 4 and 5. In this system Forms 1–3 lose the better qualified teachers; but the model is at least more simple.

Indeed, this model may be desirable even in schools which do not have Forms 6 and 7 (i.e. only go up to Form 5). Pupils usually begin to specialise in Form 4, and a system which keeps Forms 4 and 5 together ensures that class sizes are sufficiently large in the options for arts, science, agriculture, woodwork, etc.

These remarks apply to '5 + 2' systems, which may be the most proble-matic. Many countries operate '3 + 3' systems, with three years of junior secondary and three years of senior secondary schooling. In these coun-tries it is usually best to keep all junior pupils in one shift and all senior pupils in another. The arrangement ensures that staffing and other aspects of organisation are kept fairly simple.

2. How should the Timetable be Organised?

(a) General Principles

Four basic timetabling questions face administrators in double-shift systems:

i) *What is the earliest time that children can start school?* The answer chiefly depends on the time it takes children to reach school. In some societies children travel for up to two hours. If school com-mences at 7.15 am, the children have to leave home very early, perhaps without breakfast. In other societies, children only have to travel for 20 minutes or less, and school can begin earlier.

An additional problem in some countries is that the early mornings are rather cold. This applies not only to countries in the

far north and the far south of the world, but also to all moun-
tainous countries.

ii) *How frequent, and how long, should be the breaks within sessions?*
Because of the pressures of time, many double-shift systems allow
only one break during each session, though some fit in two
breaks. The breaks generally last for 15 to 20 minutes.

iii) *How much time is needed for the transition between shifts?* Most
schools allow 20 to 30 minutes, though some allow more and
others allow less. A short change-over period saves time, and
therefore allows the morning session to start later and the afternoon session to finish earlier. But change-over periods that are
too short are also chaotic. Also, a reasonably long period is needed when afternoon-session children are prohibited from entering
the school compound until the morning session has completed its
classes. Otherwise, afternoon children hang around outside the
school gate, perhaps causing problems for other people in the
neighbourhood.

iv) *What is the latest time by which classes must end?* The answer
depends on the nature of the community and the environment.
Most communities consider it desirable for children to be home
before dark. But it may be difficult to adjust going-home times to
fit the time of nightfall in different seasons; and urban areas may
have reasonable lighting, which makes the deadline less urgent.

Schools in Islamic countries must also be sensitive to the
times of prayer. It may be especially important for pupils to be
home in time for the prayers at dusk.

(b) Specific Examples

(i) End-on Systems
Most of this book is concerned with 'end-on' systems of shift schooling.
As explained in Chapter 1, this means that one group of pupils concludes
its lessons before another starts. This is the most common form of shift
system.

A typical daily timetable for a double-shift primary school in this system might be as shown in Table 5. This seems a good schedule because the
children get two breaks, both of which have a reasonable duration. It has
been made possible by the early start.

However, in some societies a starting time of 7.35 am is considered unreasonably early for both pupils and teachers. In Imo State of Nigeria, for example, classes do not commence until 8.00 am. Because they must finish at 12.45 and fit in four hours and 25 minutes of teaching time, children in double-shift schools have only one break lasting 20 minutes. This contrasts with the timetable in single-shift schools, which allocates one break of 40 minutes and another of 15 minutes. The result, according to one observer, is that pupils in double-shift schools spend too much time inactively at their desks:

> One can see that it is sitting and listening for most of the time, and the pupils easily get bored. The only organised activity is the physical education lesson, which often is haphazard because many playgrounds are too small. The afternoon session is not much better because most pupils are worn out before coming to school....

This comment emphasises the value of two breaks, even if they require the school day to start earlier.

Table 5: Typical Timetable for an End-on Double-Shift Primary School

Morning Shift:	Guidance & Extra-Curricular Activities	7.30 – 8.00
	Lesson 1	8.00 – 8.35
	Lesson 2	8.35 – 9.10
	Lesson 3	9.10 – 9.45
	Break	9.45 – 10.00
	Lesson 4	10.00 – 10.35
	Lesson 5	10.35 – 11.10
	Break	11.10 – 11.25
	Lesson 6	11.25 – 12.00
	Lesson 7	12.00 – 12.35
Afternoon Shift:	Lesson 1	1.00 – 1.35
	Lesson 2	1.35 – 2.10
	Lesson 3	2.10 – 2.45
	Break	2.45 – 3.00
	Lesson 4	3.00 – 3.35
	Lesson 5	3.35 – 4.10
	Break	4.10 – 4.25
	Lesson 6	4.25 – 5.00
	Lesson 7	5.00 – 5.35
	Guidance & Extra-Curricular Activities	5.35 – 6.00

(ii) Overlapping Systems

Alternatively, schools may operate overlapping shifts. Students arrive and leave at different times, and pupils of different shifts are on the school compound together.

One example of an overlapping shift system used in Indonesia was given in Box 3 in Chapter 1. The first shift operated from 8.15 am to 3.10 pm, and the second shift operated from 9.35 am to 4.30 pm. Between 9.35 am and 3.10 pm, all students are on the compound together. During this period sufficient space is found by (i) using every single room – including the assembly hall, library, laboratories, workshops, etc., (ii) using fields or other open spaces for physical education and agriculture classes, and (iii) if necessary holding some lessons under a tree or in some similar location.

Chapter 1 also mentioned a slightly more complicated model used in Malawi. This model allows for the fact that the daily timetable for children in different standards (grades) has different durations. The daily schedule is shown in Table 6.

Table 6: Timetable in an Overlapping Double-Shift System

Begin School Day										End School Day	
7.00am	7.30	8.00	9.00	10.00	10.40	11.00	12.00	1.05pm	2.00	3.00	4.30
Std 2 arrives	Stds 1, 6, 7, 8 arrive				Stds 1, 2 leave Stds 3, 4, 5 arrive			Stds 6, 7, 8 leave			Stds 3, 4, 5 leave

The system used in the Indonesian school is the more simple of the two. The chief *advantages* of this type of system are:

■ Students and staff feel that they belong to a single institution. There is less separation between the shifts. When necessary, the whole school can be assembled in one place at one time.

■ Staff can be used more flexibly to teach pupils of both shifts. Timetabling is therefore simplified, and it is easier to give pupils in different shifts equal access to particularly good teachers.

■ Staff find it easier to liaise with each other for subject meetings, ordering of supplies, coordination of examinations, etc..

■ Students are available at a common time for sports competitions, choir practice, etc..

- Students are less likely to feel disadvantaged if they are in one shift rather than the other.
- The school day starts later than it would in an end-on shift system. It also finishes earlier. More time is available for staff meetings and extra-curricular activities at the end of the school day.

The chief *disadvantages* of the system of overlapping shifts used in the Indonesian model are:

- The school compound is very congested during the overlap period. This may cause confusion, and may even be a safety hazard.
- If extra buildings are constructed to accommodate students during peak times, the financial savings of double-shift schooling are reduced.
- If extra buildings are not constructed, then some students have to study under trees, etc.. Learning conditions may be unsatisfactory.
- Physical education, agriculture and other lessons which are held outside have to be scheduled for the hottest time of day.
- If it rains, students who are learning outside have to come inside. There may not be any space for them, even in the corridors.
- The fact that students arrive and leave at different times of day may seem untidy and disruptive.

The Malawian model does not have so many advantages, since the students in Standards 1 and 2 leave when the students in Standards 3, 4 and 5 arrive. However, it does mean that the buildings are released. Without such a system, in many Malawian schools pupils would simply have to study outside. This is particularly problematic when the sun is intense or when it is raining. The system improves conditions for learning, and reduces absenteeism.

Table 7 shows perhaps the most intensive possible type of system, having four overlapping shifts. The timetable is organised around use of classrooms (as opposed to laboratories or open areas for physical education). The four groups of students have been scheduled in turn to take their lessons in the classrooms, and engage in other activities either before or after their classroom time. This timetable allows the classrooms to be in constant use from 7.00 am to 7.40 pm. There are no breaks in classroom use for recess or change-over between sessions: as soon as one group of pupils moves out, the next moves in. Most other systems allow breaks between blocks of lesson time, so make less intensive use of classrooms.

Table 7: Timetable from a Philippines Secondary School (Form 2) showing Quadruple-Shift System

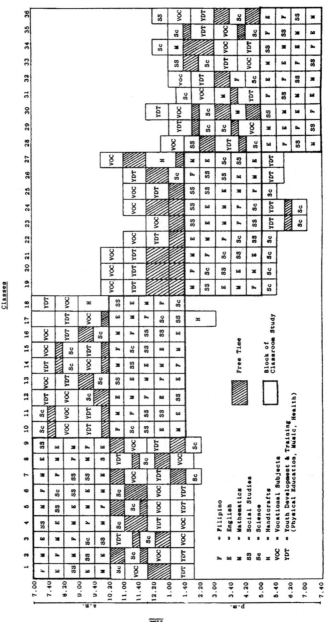

Preparation of such a timetable is, of course, very complex. This one was done by hand, but ideally should have been done by computer. The particular school whose timetable has been reproduced here is in the Philippines. It has 36 streams and 8,300 pupils! This enrolment is larger than that in many universities, and one aspect of the school is similar to that of a university, for pupils are permitted to arrive and leave according to their own schedules. There is no fixed time at which everybody begins and ends the school day.

Some other features of this timetable are also worth highlighting:

- All classroom lessons last for 40 minutes, but many other lessons last for 60 minutes, i.e. one and a half periods. If there is no immediate lesson following, the students take a break. Students break at different times according to their own specific timetables.

- Although at first glance it appears that the last shift does not get so much classroom time as the other shifts, this is not actually the case. The last shift gets the same total number of lessons, though some of the classroom lessons are held in laboratories or other places, and are scattered among the periods before the block of classroom time.

- Because of the variable times of breaks, the compound is often noisy. To reduce this problem, the classrooms have been put at the top of a four-storey building so that there is less disturbance from the noise below.

- On the other hand, variation in the times of breaks has the advantage that pressure on the school canteen is spread out. The person who drew up the timetable noted the need for each student to have a break around lunchtime, but also noted the need to stagger these breaks.

- Some students have to take lessons in physical education (which is part of Youth Development & Training or YDT) at mid-day. They therefore become hot and sweaty, and it is difficult for them to concentrate when they return immediately to ordinary classroom work. This problem cannot easily be solved.

- Some extra-curricular activities are fitted into the school day after classes, but most take place on Saturday mornings. The fact that all students are free on Saturday mornings allows formation of teams from different sessions, and helps foster a feeling of cohesion and school identity. However, students only come on Saturday mornings when they are involved in a particular activity. This means that the whole school is never in the same place at the same time. It would in any case be impossible on a small campus.

■ Apart from this school timetable, there is another for adult education. Adult classes operate from 5.30 pm to 8.30 pm, so the facilities are used even more intensively than is indicated by the school timetable!

Box 14: Different Systems for Different Seasons?

Regions which are distant from the equator have wide seasonal variations in the number of hours of daylight. Administrators usually prefer schools to close in time for children to get home before darkness. During the winter months, end-on double-shift schools find it difficult to complete their lessons in time.

One solution is to operate an overlapping instead of end-on shift system. However, administrators aware of the disadvantages of overlapping shifts might be unenthusiastic about making this a permanent arrangement.

In this case, an alternative solution might be a compromise. Schools could operate end-on shifts when daylight hours are long, and overlapping shifts when daylight hours are short. The mixture of systems might seem untidy; but with careful organisation it could be quite workable.

3. Conclusions

The choice of school structure and timetable may be partly determined by specific constraints on individual administrators. For example, safety regulations may prohibit administrators from having too many children on a school compound at once, and may therefore require and end-on rather than an overlapping shift system. Alternatively, the need to avoid pupils' travel during the hours of darkness may require an overlapping rather than an end-on system. Each country has its own regulations and specific circumstances.

The choice of school structure and timetable may also depend on administrators' personal preferences. The first part of this chapter presented six ways that the classes of a six-grade primary school could be divided between morning and afternoon shifts. Each option has both advantages and disadvantages. The final choice of system depends on the weight that individuals give to these advantages and disadvantages. Similar obser-vations apply to the choice between end-on and overlapping shifts.

It is therefore impossible to recommend a single 'best' system. Individual administrators must explore the options and decide for themselves.

Chapter 7

Staffing and Management

Introduction of double-shift systems may raise major questions of staffing and management. Policy-makers have to decide whether staff should be shared among shifts, and practitioners have to find ways to make systems work efficiently and effectively. Management is particularly challenging in overlapping shift systems.

1. Staffing Double-Shift Systems

(a) Headteachers
In some countries double-session schools have only one headteacher, but in other countries they have two. Which type of system is better?

The answer to this question depends on the viewpoint of the observer, for each type of system has good and bad sides. The advantages of one system are mirrored as disadvantages in the other.

Advantages of having only one headteacher:

■ The headteacher can guide the operation of the whole school. She/he can transfer pupils and staff from one session to another, can supervise maintenance of facilities, can avoid duplication of purchases for morning and afternoon sessions, and can encourage the growth of an overall school spirit.

■ The morning session might be more prestigious. Education authorities might find themselves pressed to appoint the best headteachers to morning sessions, leaving the afternoon sessions with the second-best staff. This is avoided if there is only one headteacher.

■ Parents who have children in both sessions can approach a single headteacher to discuss problems.

■ The school has more flexibility in class organisation. For example, it would be difficult for a school with two headteachers to have

Grades 2, 4 and 6 studying in the morning and Grades 1, 3 and 5 studying in the afternoon. Such a system would lack continuity, for headteachers would "lose" their pupils when they were promoted each year to the other session, and would then "regain" them the year after.

■ If separate sessions each have their own headteachers, the education authorities have to find a large number of appropriate individuals for these senior posts. If both sessions are combined under one head, the demand for talented headteachers is not so great. The system is less threatened by limitations in the supply of good leaders.

Disadvantages of having only one headteacher:

■ The working hours may be very long – from the beginning of the morning session to the end of the afternoon session. The long day could be very exhausting, and the headteacher might not do the job well.

■ In most systems, the salary for a headteacher of a large school is greater than the salary for a headteacher of a small school. In addition, supplementary payments might be necessary to compen-sate for the long working hours; and in large schools it is essential to appoint deputy headteachers. The system might be more costly than the alternative of having two lower-level headteachers for separate sessions.

■ Headteachers in charge of both sessions have many staff and pupils, and cannot know individuals so well. Headteachers of separate sessions can know their teachers and pupils better.

■ The number of promotion posts is smaller. A system which has separate headteachers for separate sessions has a larger number of promotion posts.

These advantages and disadvantages have been presented here from the angle of a single headteacher for a whole school. In most cases, the opposite advantages and disadvantages apply to systems which have separate headteachers for each session. The decision on which system is most appropriate will depend on the preferences of the education authorities concerned.

Box 15: Pairing Headteachers – Tips from an Educational Administrator

When double-session schools have separate headteachers for each session, the schools often suffer from poorly organised maintenance of buildings and equipment. Headteachers may also find it difficult to liaise over the employment of ancillary staff.

One experienced administrator in Hong Kong uses two strategies to reduce these problems:

- Knowing the personalities of her staff, she avoids placing two strongly competitive headteachers in the same school. She looks for one individual with strong leadership qualities, and then for another person who will accept the leadership of the first one.
- She instructs the headteachers to draw up clear divisions of responsibility. For example, one may take charge of typists while the other takes charge of cleaners, maintenance and security.

(b) Teachers

Chapters 1 and 3 pointed out variations in systems for utilisation of teachers. Staff may teach in:

- only one session,
- the whole of one session and part of another,
- in part of two (or more) sessions, or
- in the whole of two (or more) sessions.

The choice of system partly depends on (i) whether or not there is a shortage of teachers, (ii) whether or not the teachers' union agrees that staff should work in more than one session, (iii) whether the sessions are short or long, and (iv) whether schools have one headteacher for all sessions or separate headteachers for separate sessions. Sharing of teachers is particularly common in triple-shift systems because the sessions are short. Sharing is less common when separate sessions have separate headteachers, because the framework imposes practical difficulties.

The extent of teacher sharing also depends on the specialisms of the staff. For example, while there is usually enough work in single sessions for teachers of English, mathematics and social studies, this is less likely to be true for teachers of music, home economics and technical drawing. Specialist teachers are often asked to take classes in the second half of morning sessions and the first half of afternoon sessions.

Staff may also work across sessions when supervising extra-curricular activities. For example, pupils from both/all sessions may jointly participate in football matches, music competitions, athletics, field expeditions, etc..

Box 16: How do Teachers view Double-Shift Systems?

The attitudes of teachers are of course a crucial determinant of the success or fail-ure of double-shift systems. If teachers like or are at least prepared to cooperate with the systems, then the machinery can work smoothly. But if teachers feel over-worked, inadequately compensated and professionally frustrated, then the inno-vation is unlikely to be successful.

This highlights the need for policy-makers to be realistic in their expectations. Many teachers like half-day schooling because they retain the same basic salary but have more free time for their own affairs. Teachers may also like the opportu-nity to increase their incomes through extra teaching in a second shift. However, teachers sometimes feel frustrated by the professional constraints that double shifts impose, and staff in tropical countries are unenthusiastic about teaching on hot afternoons.

(c) Ancillary Staff

Many double-shift schools which have separate teachers for separate shifts nevertheless have single teams of typists, cleaners, nightwatchmen, cooks, messengers and other ancillary staff. This may permit a substantial saving of salaries.

This type of system may require special arrangements to ensure that duties are covered appropriately. Take, for example, a country in which normal working hours for clerical staff are 8.00 to 4.00 pm. A double-ses-sion school might operate from 7.30 am to 5.30 pm. This implies:

- either that the school office is closed for part of the school day (and that the afternoon session suffers more severely than the morning one),
- or that the clerical staff themselves work on an overlapping shift system, with one or more staff arriving early and then leaving early, while others arrive later and leave later.

2. Managing Double-Shift Systems

Many of the challenges and techniques of management have already been mentioned. However, it is useful to make several additional points.

single shift

end-on
double shift

multiple
overlapping
shift

The problems of school management greatly increase when extra shifts are added. Overlapping shift systems are the most difficult to manage.

It will have become obvious that management tasks are more challenging in double-shift schools than in single-shift ones. This is true in end-on double-shift schools, but is even more true of overlapping double-shift schools. Chapter 6 highlighted a school in the Philippines that had 8,300 pupils in four overlapping shifts. Management of this school must be an extremely difficult task.

This fact has implications for recruitment and training. Before a double-shift system is introduced or extended, authorities would be wise to check whether they have a sufficient supply of appropriate people to run the schools. They might also wish to organise short training courses to discuss ways of:

- deploying teachers between shifts,
- deploying ancillary staff between shifts,
- promoting a feeling of school unity
  in institutions divided between two or more shifts,
- managing movement of students, especially
  - in end-on shifts at the times of change-over, and
  - in overlapping systems when two or more groups are on the campus together,
- ensuring that extra-curricular activities are given appropriate attention,
- adapting the main curriculum (if it is necessary to reduce daily teaching time), and
- liaising with parents over such matters as nutrition, safety in travel to and from school (especially if the shift system requires travel during hours of darkness), rotation of shifts, etc..

Such training courses might last for only a week, or they might be longer. Leadership could be provided by headteachers and their assistants who have themselves run double-shift schools and have found solutions to the difficulties.

Chapter 8

Quality

Chapter 4 pointed out that double-shift schools are not necessarily qualitatively inferior to single-shift schools. Indeed, if the choice is between single-shift schools with huge classes and congested facilities or double-shift schools with smaller classes and a more personal atmos-phere, the double-shift schools may actually be better.

Nevertheless, educators raise many legitimate concerns about the quality of double-shift schooling. Accordingly, this chapter focuses on ways that their concerns may be met. It looks first at the main curriculum, then at extra-curricular activities, and thirdly at links between school and home.

1. The Main Curriculum

As noted in Chapter 4, double-shift systems are threatened by many qualitative problems. Seven possible strategies to deal with these problems are particularly worth highlighting.

1. *Increase the number of school days.* One way to compensate for a shortened school day is to increase the number of days in the academic year. Thus double-shift schools in Senegal have 10 extra school days in the academic year, and double-shift schools in Hong Kong operate on alternate Saturday mornings.
2. *Improve teaching methods.* Arrangements to lengthen the school term and week will generate little benefit if the quality of teaching is poor and if children are bored. Authorities should therefore try hard to ensure that lessons are lively and meaningful. Improvements may be achieved through strengthened supervision and support systems, pre-service and in-service training, better teaching aids, etc.. These inputs are needed in all systems, but may be especially desirable in double-shift systems in order to compensate for the constraints that double shifts impose.

3. *Improve the efficiency of the system.* In many systems, official teaching hours are rather different from actual teaching hours. Especially in the rural parts of poor countries, teachers who are inadequately supervised start school late and finish school early. The real school day, therefore, is even shorter than it appears at first sight. Authorities may be able to improve efficiency by strengthening supervision. If distances prevent central authorities from checking rural schools, the task can perhaps be delegated to community members on Boards of Management.

4. *Encourage out-of-school learning.* The classroom is not the only place in which students learn. Even in traditional single-shift systems, pupils are usually given homework. In double-shift systems they can be given more homework. Of course, homework needs to be corrected. But this does not always have to be done by the teachers. Education authorities can design self-teaching materials. Alternatively, they can design materials for group work and peer correction. Research has demonstrated that pupils often learn a great deal when they correct the work of their peers. Peer-teaching can therefore be an effective educational strategy as well as a way to reduce the workload for the teachers.

   Authorities may also invest in public libraries, and may encourage establishment of study areas in mosques, churches, temples, community halls, etc.. The facilities may cater for pupils whose homes are too crowded or noisy for private study, but who cannot stay on the school compound because it is occupied by the other shift.

5. *Give schools at least one extra room* which is not in constant use for regular lessons. The room can then be used for remedial or other work outside the hours of a particular shift. Many teachers stay on the school compound after the morning shift or come long before they have to commence lessons for the afternoon shift. The teachers are often happy to conduct extra individual and group work with pupils who need it; but they need space to do it in.

6. *Ensure that teachers make full use of classroom walls* for display purposes. Good use of walls to display supplementary lesson material and pupils' work is one of the key indicators of a lively and effective teaching process. Posters and other colourful items brighten the atmosphere, encourage pupils' sense of belonging to their classrooms, and promote learning outside lesson time.

Wall space in double-shift schools is often neglected. Because classrooms are used by two or more sets of pupils, teachers and pupils have less feeling of ownership of those classrooms. They may fear that displays put up by one set of pupils will be damaged by the other set. Teachers may also fear that wall displays will confuse pupils of the other shift. This is especially likely when the different shifts cater for pupils of different grades. Thus, if a classroom caters for Grade 4 in the morning and Grade 1 in the afternoon, teachers may fear that the Grade 4 pupils will find Grade 1 wall displays too juvenile, and that the Grade 1 children will find the Grade 4 displays too complex.

Teachers may also be sensitive about each others' work. If one teacher puts up many displays and the other puts up nothing, inter-personal relationships may be uncomfortable. Ideally, a good example by one teacher would improve the work of the other. But sometimes the good teacher gets discouraged, and in the end nothing is put up by either teacher.

Failure to put up wall displays is a missed opportunity for quali-tative improvement. Especially when the two sessions serve pupils of

Wall displays brighten the classroom atmosphere and promote learning outside lesson time. When classrooms are shared by two or more shifts, teachers should divide up the wall space between them. Children can learn a lot by looking at the displays of the other shifts.

the same grade, children can learn a lot from each others' displays. In this respect, the double-shift system could actually be beneficial. The morning shift of Grade 4 may gain reinforcement by looking at the wall displays of the afternoon shift of Grade 4 as well as by looking at their own.

7. *Ensure that staff rooms are large enough.* Ideally, all teachers should have their own desks, whether they work in the morning or the afternoon sessions. If staff have their own desks, they will be more willing to come early or stay late, to undertake thorough preparation of lessons, etc.. If space is so constrained that morning staff must share desks with afternoon staff, the authorities should at least try to provide a few spare desks for displaced teachers.

Box 17: The Extra Problems of Inspecting Double-Shift Schools

Double-shift schools are sometimes 'short-changed' in inspections. This happens for two reasons:

- In many systems, the morning and afternoon shifts are considered part of a single school supervised by one headteacher. The schools are often very large, and it is difficult to assemble correspondingly large teams of inspectors to conduct full evaluations. The inspectorate may neglect double-shift schools, instead concentrating on smaller schools which are less demanding.
- The hours of schooling may not match the normal hours for inspections. For example, the normal working hours for inspectors might be 8.00 am to 4.00 pm. Inspectors could easily assess the morning shift, but might neglect at least the second half of the afternoon shift.

This type of problem requires careful attention from the authorities. It can easily be solved by making a special effort to form large teams and by adjusting the inspectors' working hours when necessary. But it may require this special effort.

---

2.   Extra-Curricular Activities

Chapter 4 also highlighted the problems facing extra-curricular activities in double-shift schools. Table 8 presents some possible solutions to these problems.

Table 8: Extra-Curricular Activities – Problems and Possible Solutions

Problems	Solutions
School compounds are too crowded. There is no space for extra-curricular activities.	Conduct activities outside school compounds. Use community facilities for football, drama, music, etc.. Organise visits to museums, factories, country parks and so on.
Drama, group music and sports teams cannot be formed for the whole school because when some pupils are free, the others are studying.	(a) Designate one day a week on which morning classes finish an hour early and afternoon classes start an hour late; or (b) hold activities on Saturday mornings (if there are no classes that day).
Teachers who serve more than one shift have to rush from one shift to the next.	Ask senior pupils, parents or other members of the community to supervise extra-curricular activities.
The school compound is large enough, but some activities (e.g. music practice) disturb pupils who are studying	Find a place outside the compound or, if sufficiently prosperous, construct a sound-proof room.

This list shows that few obstacles to effective extra-curricular activities in double-shift schools are insurmountable. If staff make the effort to find ways round the obstacles, extra-curricular activities in double-shift schools can be at least as good as those in single-shift schools. Indeed in some respects they may be even better, for, as noted in Chapter 4, the larger population of double-shift schools makes it easier to justify investments in basketball courts, musical instruments, sports equipment, etc..

3. Links between School and Home

The home environment is a third determinant of educational quality. If children spend more hours at home because of a double-session system, the home environment becomes more important.

This fact implies that double-shift schools may need especially strong Parent-Teacher Associations and other bodies for liaison between school and home. These bodies need to address such questions as:

■ *Use of Out-of-School Time.* Do pupils waste their time hanging around on the streets or watching too much television when they could be doing other things? How can parents help children with

---

Box 18: Using Saturdays for Extra-Curricular Activities

Many double-shift schools have little time for extra-curricular activities on Mondays to Fridays. They therefore make use of Saturday mornings.

This system has the strong advantage that sports teams, Scout and Guide troops, school choirs, etc. can be recruited from all shifts. Apart from enlarging the pool of talent, the arrangement helps to promote pupils' identity with the whole school rather than with just their particular shifts.

One problem, is that school compounds may not be large enough to accommodate all pupils at the same time. To deal with this difficulty, many schools organise activities in rotation. Staff only ask pupils to come when the pupils are actually involved in activities on that particular day.

---

their studies? Homework may become even more important in a double-shift system than in a single-shift system.

- *Sleeping Times.* When should the afternoon-shift pupils do their homework? Should they do it the same evening, even though they may be tired and may be distracted by other family activities? If so, they may go to bed late, knowing that they can also get up late since they do not have to go to school until mid-day. Or should the children go to bed early, and do their homework the following morning? If they do this, their minds may be fresher; but there may be fewer adults available to supervise and help them.

- *Waking Times.* Teachers often complain that because the morning shift starts quite early, children come to school without having eaten proper breakfasts. Pupils in the morning shift often need to get up before anybody else in the family, with the result that they are inadequately cared for.

- *Changing Shifts.* In order to make the system more fair, some education authorities like to alternate pupils between shifts. It is essential in these cases for the authorities to inform parents and other family members.

Many of these measures to improve quality are of course desirable in *all* systems; but they may be especially important in double-shift systems.

PART IV

Chapter 9

Alternative Models and Cost-Effectiveness

After going through this book, readers may have found that the issues associated with double-shift schooling are more complex than they had appeared at first sight. The work of policy-makers is therefore difficult. Education authorities have to balance a wide range of competing factors, and must find strategies which are not only cost-effective but also politically acceptable.

This chapter begins by noting the need for policy-makers to identify priorities. In the technical language introduced in Chapter 2, this requires them to determine the 'utilities' of alternative uses for resources. Secondly, the chapter summarises the evidence on double-shift schooling and cost-effectiveness. The third section notes the possibility of different policies for different levels of education. Finally, the chapter comments on the social context for policy making and on various strategies for implementation of reform.

1. Identifying Priorities

Policy-makers are constantly faced by dilemmas in the allocation of scarce resources. When choosing between alternative models for school systems, how can policy-makers identify priorities?

The answer to this question of courses lie in the sphere of politics as well as in the domain of cost analysis. This book cannot explore in detail the complexities of decision making in all settings, but it can outline some elements. In connection with double-shift schooling, it is helpful to commence with an analogy.

The analogy concerns motor cars. Single-shift schooling may be compared with an expensive car, and double-shift schooling with a more modest one. The expensive car is more comfortable both for its passengers (the public) and its driver (the teachers). Anybody who has a choice would therefore prefer the expensive car – particularly if that individual does not personally have to meet the cost. But a modest car may fulfil the basic needs of transportation quite adequately, and may be much more appropriate to the income levels of particular individuals. In the same way, double-shift schooling may meet the basic needs of education quite adequately, and may be more appropriate to the income levels of particular countries.

Single-shift schooling is like an expensive car, and double-shift schooling is like a modest car. The expensive car is luxurious, but both vehicles carry their passengers where they want to go. Expensive cars do not necessarily give good value for money. For many people, modest cars represent the most appropriate investment.

Expanding on this metaphor, an individual trying to decide whether to buy an expensive or a modest car would have to:

- assess the strength of available financial resources,
- think about the effectiveness of the car in meeting transportation and other needs,
- identify alternative uses for the money that could be saved by buying a modest instead of an expensive car, and finally
- decide on priorities.

Decisions on investment in school systems can be approached in the same way.

- If governments are poor, it may be totally impossible even to think about the single-shift schooling. Only if the governments are reasonably rich will they have a choice (unless instead they decide to limit the coverage of education so that only a few children go to school and most are excluded).

- On the question of effectiveness, this book has pointed out that there may be differences in the outcomes of alternative school models, but that the differences are unlikely to be great.
- Alternative uses for resources will always exist – both within education and in other sectors.
- The real question, therefore, is on priorities. Governments have to decide whether they wish to opt for the extra luxury and prestige of a single-shift school system or whether to retain the more modest double-shift system and use the money they have saved for other projects.

From this analysis it will be obvious that the fact that most rich countries have expensive education systems does not necessarily mean that their model is the most appropriate for every country. Policy-makers should look for the model which best meets priority needs within the constraints of financial stringency.

2.   Double-Shift Schooling and Cost-Effectiveness

The points made in this book about cost-effectiveness deserve summary and emphasis. Chapter 2 noted that a cost-effective model of education is not necessarily the one which produces the best quality product; nor is it necessarily the cheapest. It is the one which gives the best value for money within the budgetary constraints of the purchaser.

Box 19: Decision-Making and Utilities

In the technical language introduced in Chapter 2, the desirability of an object may be expressed as a 'utility' value. A rich person may decide to buy an expensive car because that person can easily afford it and does not have other more urgent needs. A person with a modest income may also decide to buy the car, even if the person has to make sacrifices elsewhere in order to find the money. Both individuals place a higher utility value On the car than on other things which might be purchased with their money.

   Similar decisions may be made by governments. Governments of rich countries might decide that they want single-shift schooling because they can easily afford it and do not have more urgent claims on their resources. Governments of poorer countries might also decide that they want to have single-shift schooling, even if they have to sacrifice other forms of investment. This decision to give priority to single-shift schooling reflects the high utility that the governments place on single-shift schooling, and the lower utility that they place on the alternative uses for their resources.

The book has shown that double-shift systems can be highly cost-effective. They can permit substantial financial savings, and do not necessarily cause a decline in quality. And even when introduction of double-shift schooling does cause some loss of quality, the benefits of reduced unit costs and of larger enrolments may outweigh the cost implied by the loss of quality.

As noted above, these facts will of course weigh heavily in the policy making process. However, education authorities cannot simply assume that double-shift systems will operate cost-effectively. They must take specific steps to achieve the goal. Such steps should include:

1. *Choice of model.* This book has been mainly concerned with 'end-on' systems of double-shift schooling. This relatively simple model is the one found in the widest range of countries. However, governments might wish to examine the system of overlapping shifts or other models highlighted in Chapter 1.

2. *Management structures.* Double-shift schools present strong managerial challenges. Triple-shift systems are more complex than double or single-shift systems, and overlapping systems are more complex than end-on systems. Authorities need to pay attention to managerial structures and to recruitment and training of good personnel. It may be desirable to organise special short courses from time to time.

3. *Hours of schooling.* Double-shift systems should be designed so that sacrifices of time for both lessons and extra-curricular activities are not too serious. This requires careful examination not only of the school day but also of the school week and the school year. It may be possible to compensate for loss of time in a normal school day by making better use of Saturday mornings and by extending the length of school terms.

4. *Out-of-school learning.* The impact of shortened teaching time can also be reduced by encouraging out-of-school learning. Teachers might be requested to give more homework assignments, and families can be guided on ways to help their children do the assignments. In addition, good textbooks and special self-instructional materials may be prepared.

5. *Use of teachers.* Education authorities have to decide whether to restrict teachers to individual sessions or whether to ask them to teach in double sessions. The decision will depend on (i) the supply of competent teachers, (ii) the views of the teachers' union, (iii) estimates of

the impact of teacher tiredness on the quality of teaching, and (iv) the extent to which extra work is remunerated by extra pay.

6. *Extra rooms.* It was pointed out that availability of one or two extra rooms can provide considerable benefits. Teachers can use the rooms for remedial and other extra tuition, and pupils can use the rooms for doing homework. Education authorities would need to assess their budgetary and physical space constraints to decide whether it is possible to construct a few extra rooms in each school.

Box 20: End-on or Overlapping Shifts?

The system of end-on shifts is the most popular, and has the strongest potential for budgetary savings. However, some education authorities consider the model of overlapping shifts preferable. It does not save so much money, and it can create major management problems; but the model does have some attractive features.

The relative strengths of each model have been carefully appraised in Jamaica. One report recommended an 'extended day' in which the first shift would operate from 7.30 am to 1.30 pm, and the second shift would operate from 9.00 am to 3.00 pm. The report pointed out that:

> careful time tabling of classes and scheduling of break times for each set of students would allow sole use of the school facilities by each shift for approximately 2.5 hours per day. For the remainder of the school day, the facilities would be shared. Classes in physical education, art, music, science or other special subjects would occupy the facilities designed for these purposes, thus leaving rooms free for other classes.

As noted in Chapter 6, one major problem of overlapping shifts is congestion. In some countries, overlapping systems have been replaced by end-on systems because the authorities have been worried about safety.

However, overlapping systems also have strong advantages. At one point each day all teachers and students are on the compound together, so can have a stronger sense of belonging to a single school. The fact that all teachers can work in both shifts makes timetabling more flexible and encourages coordination of curricula. Also, more time is available at the end of the second shift for meetings and extra-curricular activities. Finally, students are less likely to feel disadvantaged when attending one shift rather than the other.

According to the Jamaican report, capital costs for the extended-day system would be 24% less than those for the single-shift system. Costs would be 32% less in a system of end-on double shifts, but the report felt that the educational disadvantages outweighed the financial savings.

7. *Use of other community facilities.* When school compounds are really too congested, it may be possible to use other community facilities. Teachers could be encouraged to use public sports fields, libraries, halls, etc..

In summary, double-shift schooling may be highly cost-effective. However, cost-effectiveness is not achieved automatically: administrators must take specific steps to achieve the goal. If administrators are unable or unwilling to take these steps, then the cost-effectiveness of double-shift schooling will be threatened and the model will become less desirable.

3.   Different Policies for Different Levels?

This book has also pointed out firstly that junior sections of individual schools may be treated differently from senior sections, and secondly that primary schools may be treated differently from secondary schools. It is useful to summarise and supplement previous discussion.

(a) Junior vs Senior Sections

Chapter 6 noted that in Zambia, for example, Grades 1–4 are treated differently from Grades 5–7. This is chiefly because the hours of schooling are shorter in junior than in senior primary school. Even triple sessions may be fitted into daylight hours at the junior level, but such scheduling is impossible at the senior level. Separate treatment of the two levels improves efficiency and gives the authorities greater flexibility. The fact that senior forms never have triple shifts, and in many cases do not even have double shifts, may be especially important to pupils taking public examinations.

The chapter also noted parallels in secondary schools. One policy variation concerns Forms 6 and 7. Some schools schedule these classes across shifts so that highly qualified teachers that normally teach these senior classes are also available for the more junior classes of both shifts. Authorities may also decide to treat Forms 1 to 3 differently from Forms 4 and 5.

Finally, Chapter 5 highlighted the dangers inherent in the Trinidad & Tobago model in which junior secondary schools (Forms 1–3) had double sessions but full secondary schools (Forms 1–5) had single sessions. The mere existence of the two types of institution was inequitable, for pupils admitted to Form 1 of full secondary schools had a better chance of proceeding to Form 5 than did children who entered junior secondary schools and who had later to compete for a Form 4 place in a separate institution. The inequity was made worse by requiring only the junior secondary schools to operate double sessions. Research has demonstrated at least partial correlation between academic success and socio-economic background. The system in Trinidad & Tobago discriminated against low socio-economic families.

(b) Primary versus Secondary Schools

Policy-makers may also treat primary schools as a whole differently from secondary schools as a whole. For example, they may decide to operate double shifts at one level but not at another.

One factor is that economic savings may be greater at the secondary level, for secondary schools usually have more costly buildings and facilities. Also, secondary school students are more likely to use their spare time for productive economic activities when not in school. These two facts suggest that if authorities wish either (i) to introduce double-shifts at one level but not both, or (ii) to phase out double-shifts from one level but not both, then it is more desirable to have double-shifts in secondary than primary schools.

However, an alternative approach points to an opposite conclusion. Research in Singapore has shown that secondary schools are more likely to take advantage of the opportunities offered by a single-session system than are primary schools. The research found that when selected schools were converted from double-session to single-session, secondary school pupils spent about twice as much time in after-school activities, thus making better use of their school facilities. The chief reasons were that (i) secondary staff responded more readily to the increased opportunities, and (ii) because the secondary pupils were older and more independent, they were better able to organise their own activities.

The opposing nature of these possibilities makes it difficult to set out firm recommendations on whether double-shift schooling is more desirable (or less undesirable) at primary rather than secondary level. Once again, policy-makers need to assess factors in their own contexts.

4. The Social Context of Policy Making

Finally, it must be recognised that double-shift schooling is rarely popular with the general public. It may not matter how cost-effective a model may be if social and political forces are against it. In almost all countries the public assumes that double-shift schooling is qualitatively inferior to single-shift schooling, even when there is no empirical evidence to support such an assumption.

Moreover, the fact that double-shift schooling can extend access and therefore improve equity is not particularly appealing to families whose children are already in school. Because they fear that their own children will suffer, these families are likely to campaign against introduction of double-shift schooling; and the fact that the innovation could assist other people's children who are not able to attend school is irrelevant to them.

This type of situation requires governments which wish to introduce or extend double-shift schooling to pay attention to certain implementation strategies.

1. *Publicity.* The authorities must explain why they consider double-shift schooling to be desirable. If they have reason to think that quality will not fall, then they must explain this fact. If they feel that quality might fall a little, but that this cost will be outweighed by the other benefits, then they must explain this fact too.

   Such publicity, it may be added, has to take many forms in order to reach all segments of the population. Rationales should be presented in official reports, in publicity brochures, in the press, in posters, and on the radio and television. Government officers must be prepared to enter dialogue with representatives of teachers' unions and community bodies. The message must be explained consistently,

---

Box 21: The Need for Publicity: Senegalese Experience

When the government of Senegal first tried to introduce double-shift schooling, it encountered major political problems. The authorities had not embarked on adequate general publicity, and initial public opposition was much stronger than the policy-makers had anticipated. The experience stressed the need for particular effort to inform:

- parents whose children were already in school,
- teachers, and
- community leaders.

The authorities found it helpful to be able to point out that (a) double-session schooling operated effectively in many other countries, and (b) the benefits in those countries generally outweighed the costs.

patiently and frequently. Omission of such publicity exercises is likely to cause reforms to fail.

In many countries, publicity is needed most strongly within the education profession rather than in the community as a whole. Inspectors in particular tend to be strongly opposed to double-shift systems. They see themselves as the guardians of quality, but are less about well informed about or interested in questions of finance.

2. *Social equity.* Double-shift schooling will also be resisted if it is seen as a system only for the lower classes. The situation in Trinidad & Tobago was highlighted above, and the example may be supplemented by another from Uganda. When double-shift schooling was introduced in Uganda during the 1960s, elite schools were exempted from the innovation. The general public immediately associated double-shift schooling with inferior-quality education, and rightly protested against the government's biased treatment. As a result, at that time double-shift schooling did not have a chance to prove its worth. If they had seriously believed in double-shift schooling, the authorities should have introduced it in the elite schools as well as in the ordinary schools. However, in the 1990s another effort was made in Uganda to promote double-shift schooling on a wide scale.

3. *Reasonably large-scale implementation.* Introduction of double-shift schooling also needs to be done on a reasonably large scale. Papua New Guinean experience is relevant in this context. The authorities decided to introduce double-shift schooling on a "pilot" basis in only two schools. Those schools felt that they had been singled out for punishment. Parents tried to transfer their children to other schools, and political pressures forced abandonment of project before it ever had a chance to succeed.

4. *Persistence.* Much initial opposition to double-shift schooling arises because people are not used to the idea. But once teachers, families and the general public adjust, they find that the system is not so bad after all. Double-sessions have existed for many years in countries as far apart as India, Nigeria and Jamaica. They are accepted as part of the system, and are no longer the focus of massive public complaint.

Further Reading

Although double-shift schools are found in many parts of the world, literature on their operation and impact is scarce. It is common to find passing reference to double shifts in official and other reports, but it is rare to find detailed analysis. Nevertheless, some relevant publications should be available in large libraries and through inter-library loans. They are listed here.

Batra, Sunil (1998): *Problems and Prospects of Double Shift Schools: A Study of Assam and Madhya Pradesh*, Centre for Education, Action and Research, Delhi. [A2/20A, Model Town, Delhi 110 009, India. E-mail: cear@vsnl.com]

> This is a very thorough and balanced study of policies and practice in two of India's states. The empirical component compares the operation of 31 double-shift schools with 15 single-shift schools, and includes interview data from headteachers, teachers, parents and students. The study argues that double shifts can be an appropriate model, but stresses the importance of good management.

Beebout, Harold Seymour (1972): 'The Production Surface for Academic Achievement: An Economic Study of Malaysian Secondary Schools', Ph.D. dissertation, University of Wisconsin, 258 pp.

> Beebout examined the academic achievement of 7,674 Form 5 students in 89 West Malaysian schools. He collected data on the number of shifts, socio-economic background, teacher qualifications, class size and several other aspects of the system. This enabled him to control for other factors in multiple regression. Malay-medium students performed more poorly in double-session than in single-session schools, but there was no significant difference in the performance of English-medium students. The dissertation is an excellent example of the techniques and complexities of cost-effectiveness analysis.

Bray, Mark (1989): 'Bisessional versus Unisessional Education: Hong Kong Policies and Practice in Comparative Perspective', *New Horizons* [Hong Kong], No.30, pp.81–88.

> The paper was prepared in the light of official proposals (later partially postponed) to phase out bisessional schooling in Hong Kong. It first describes the Hong Kong model for bisessional schooling. It then discusses the economic, educational and social issues arising from bisessional schooling. The paper suggests that official policies are based on shallow analysis, and that more careful consideration of issues might lead to a less negative attitude towards bisessional schooling.

Cheung, Wing-ming (1995): 'Micropolitics in Managing Bi-sessional Primary Schools: A Case Study of Interactions between Partner School Heads', *New Horizons in Education* [Hong Kong], No.36, pp.1–13.

> The study explored the interactions between the heads of a bi-sessional primary school in the context of their goal to achieve the school mission and a sense of school unity. One head was already in the school when the other head joined, and initially they worked harmoniously in a 'master-apprentice' relationship. Later transition in micropolitics was a bitter experience for the heads, but healthy for the school as a whole.

Chiu, Shiu-Yim (1990): 'The Administration of Bisessional Primary Schools', in Bray, Mark (ed.), *Educational Administration in Hong Kong: Personnel and Schools*, Education Paper 5, Faculty of Education, The University of Hong Kong, pp.27–38.

> Some bisessional schools in Hong Kong have two headteachers, while others have only one. The author surveyed two thirds of the bisessional schools with one headteacher and half of the schools with two headteachers. His article compares the operation of the schools. Appointment of separate headteachers created problems of coordination, militated against a feeling of school unity, and reduced sharing of resources between the sessions. However, headteachers responsible for both sessions had heavy workloads.

Clermont, C.M. & Thomas, R.M. (1985): 'Shift Systems', in Husèn, T. & Postlethwaite, T.N. (eds.), *An International Encyclopedia of Education*, Pergamon Press, Oxford, pp.4565–4567.

> The article begins by noting the wide range of terms and systems. It then focuses on 10 problems and on the ways that shift systems can help solve

them. The problems include shortage of facilities and teachers, unduly large classes, the special needs of subgroups, and the demands of work and study experiences.

Colclough, Christopher with Lewin, Keith M. (1993): *Educating all the Children: Strategies for Primary Schooling in the South*, Clarendon Press, Oxford.

This book focuses on the goal of good-quality primary schooling for all children in less developed countries. Part of the strategy for achieving that goal concerns utilisation of resources. The book discusses double shift schooling as a tool to achieve the goal. In addition to general discussion, it includes a case study of Senegal.

Farrell, J.P. & Schiefelbein, E. (1974): 'Expanding the Scope of Educational Planning: The Experience of Chile', *Interchange*, Vol.5, No.2, pp.18–30.

The researchers investigated academic achievement in 353 schools. They found no significant differences between pupils in single, double and triple shifts, and recommended extension of the shift system in order to reduce costs.

Fuller, B., Dellagnelo, L., Strath, A.., Bastos, E.S.B., Maia, M.H., de Matos, K.S.L., Portela, A.L. & Viera, S.L. (1999): 'How to Raise Children's Early Literacy? The Influence of Family, Teacher, and Classroom in Northeast Brazil', *Comparative Education Review*, Vol.43, No.1, pp.1–35.

Literacy tests for Grade 1 and 2 children were conducted in 140 schools in two states of Northeast Brazil. The researchers investigated both in-school and out-of-school determinants of achievement. They found that class size and the school's number of shifts were not related to achievement levels.

Knight, Brian (1989): *Managing School Time*, Longman, Harlow, Essex.

Knight presents a thorough analysis of the ways that school time is used in different settings. One chapter focuses on the United Kingdom, but much of the rest of the book has an international focus. The book considers not only the school day but also the school year. The study concludes with a chapter on strategies for change.

Leo-Rhynie, Elsa (1981): *Report on the Shift System in Jamaican Schools*,

School of Education, University of the West Indies, Mona, Jamaica, 118 pp.

> This is a detailed analysis of Jamaica's double-session system, which was first proposed in 1953 and then introduced in various phases during the 1960s and 1970s. A team of researchers analysed the impact of double shifts on teachers' workloads, curriculum content, teacher-pupil relationships, extra-curricular activities, and parental attitudes.

Levin, Henry M. (1983): *Cost-Effectiveness: A Primer*, Sage Publications, Beverly Hills, 167 pp.

> Levin explains in clear terms the basic procedures for conducting cost-effectiveness analysis and the related procedures for cost-benefit analysis, cost-utility analysis and cost-feasibility analysis. His examples are all taken from the education sector.

London, Norrel A. (1993): 'Planning and Implementing Education Policy in a Developing Country: A Study of the Shift System in Trinidad and Tobago', *Journal of Education Policy*, Vol.8, No.4, pp.353–364.

> Double-shift schooling was introduced in secondary schools in Trinidad & Tobago in the early 1970s in an effort to expand supply of places. However, it was controversial because the elite schools continued to operate single shifts. The government promised to phase out the double shifts, but later decided to keep them to save costs and retain the supply of places. The article analyses the technical and political reasons for the introduction of double shifts and for the failure to phase them out again.

Merrell, Russell G. (1980): A Report on Alternatives to School Building Construction, Utah State Board of Education, Salt Lake City, 52 pp.

> The Utah State Board of Education commissioned the author to find ways to reduce massive demands for school construction. Among the options discussed are double-session schooling, an extended school day, and a system of year-round-schools. The report notes that double-session schooling would substantially reduce building demands, and would not necessarily create educational problems. However, the system was not recommended because the report recognised political obstacles.

Nhundu, Tichatonga J. (2000): 'Headteacher and Teacher Perspectives of Multiple-shift Schooling Practices: A Zimbabwean Experience', *International Studies in Educational* Administration, Vol.28, No.1, pp.42–56.

A detailed survey was conducted on a sample of 47 double-shift primary and secondary schools in Zimbabwe. Double-shift schooling is more common in urban than rural areas, and is associated with former Group B (former Blacks-only) schools which are found in the poorer, high-density suburbs. Partly for this reason, perceptions towards double shifts were rather negative. However, the author points out that this may have been because of the way that the double-shift system has been implemented rather than because of inherent problems in the system.

Tsang, Mun C. (1997): 'Cost Analysis for Improved Policymaking and Evaluation', *Educational Evaluation and Policy Analysis*, Vol.19, No.4, pp.318–324.

Tsang surveys major types of cost analysis in education, gives examples of their application, and presents major lessons learned. Policies on quality basic education for all and on privatisation of schooling are given particular focus.

Windham, Douglas M. (1988): *Indicators of Educational Effectiveness and Efficiency*, project for Improving the Efficiency of Educational Systems (IEES), Florida State University, Tallahassee, 212 pp.

The IEES project primarily focuses on the education systems of Botswana, Haiti, Indonesia, Liberia, Nepal, Somalia and Yemen. Drawing on experiences in those countries, the author has prepared a very comprehensive discussion of indicators of effectiveness and efficiency. Perhaps surprisingly, the book does not devote attention to double-shift schooling. However, it contains very useful discussion on related areas and on the basic concepts of cost-effectiveness and cost-utility analysis.

Note on the Author

Mark Bray is Director of the Comparative Education Research Centre at the University of Hong Kong. He has taught in secondary schools in Kenya and Nigeria, and at the Universities of Edinburgh, Papua New Guinea and London. He has worked as a consultant in over 50 countries in Africa, Asia, the Caribbean, Europe, North America and the South Pacific for such organisations as the Asian Development Bank, the Commonwealth Secretariat, UNESCO, UNICEF and the World Bank. His other books focus on the planning, financing and sociology of education.

Address: Comparative Education Research Centre, The University of Hong Kong, Pokfulam Road, Hong Kong, China. Fax: (852) 2517 4727. E-mail: mbray@hku.hk.